The Elijah Project

The Elijah Project:
My Protector, My Provider

Cover artwork created by Matthew Reddy

Additional artwork and illustrations created by Matthew Reddy, Christina Rambo, Lisa Hardy and Andrea Polnaszek.

Graphic Designer: Lisa Hardy

Assistant to the author: Renee Wurzer

Printed in the United States of America

ISBN 978-0-578-20252-5

Dedication

Dedicated to my husband Perry who simply said: *Write it all down.* I appreciate your vision, courage, and encouragement. It's just another ordinary day in our extraordinary life. I love you!

A Note from Andrea

I received my first Amy Grant album (literally a vinyl record) when I was 12 years old. From that day on I unofficially became Amy Grant's biggest fan. My friend and I would go to the Christian bookstore the day her albums came out and listen to our cassette tapes until the tape would disintegrate. One of the many things I appreciate about Amy is the way she expresses her gratitude to everyone involved in making her albums. She didn't just say: *Thank You.* She created a tribute to each participant. Her descriptions gave me a visual of each person. Each and every person on this list shared a part of themselves which made *The Elijah Project* be what it is.

There are not adequate words… yet here is a modest attempt at gratitude.

Renee – Without you none of this would be possible. You have encouraged, supported and taken everything to the next level.

Lisa – Your gifts have allowed *The Elijah Project* books to come to life.

Christina and Matt – Thank you for contributing your artistry in the visual images that captured our hearts.

Linda – Thank you for walking with me while we taught *The Elijah Project* class at New Day Yoga.

Rhonda – Thank you for giving me the opportunity to share with the St. Joseph Hospital community.

Jodi – Thank you for inviting me to share EP with the nurses.

Diane – Thank you for inviting me to practice and perfect the journey at Jacob's Well.

Destiny, Jessica, Peggy and Tami – Thank you for not letting me slip away and investing 20 weeks in completing the *Boundaries* study with me.

All the Women – Thank you to all the women who over the years risked and vulnerably shared their stories with me as we journeyed through *The Elijah Project*.

Alexandra and John – Thank you for taking a risk by both including me in the making of *Catching Faith* and highlighting *The Elijah Project* in the film.

A2 (and company), A3, A4 – You are always my greatest cheerleaders. I ♥ you!

Mom and Dad – Thank you for giving me a solid biblical foundation, for sacrificing to give me a Christian education and for always supporting me with love.

Will, Izzy and Jael – You have sacrificed time with me, while encouraging me to keep going when I most wanted to give up.

God – You are the God!

Immediately the fire of the Lord flashed down from heaven and burned up the young bull, the wood, the stones, and the dust. It even licked up all the water in the trench![39] And when all the people saw it, they fell face down on the ground and cried out, "The Lord—he is God! Yes, the Lord is God!" – *1 Kings 18:38-39 NLT*

Table of Contents

How It Began

For 20 years I have had the privilege to walk with children, adolescents, and families through the trauma and pain of their stories. As a licensed clinical social worker, youth pastor, church community member, and administrator of Touched Twice United, I have had a bird's eye view into the hurt that happens on this broken planet. There are no easy answers and no quick fixes. My rule of thumb is to find a safe person and share your story until it becomes such a part of you that you can speak it without crying. God graciously collects all of our tears and holds them in a bottle until the day of His return. He will protect and provide in the midst of our pain.

The Elijah Project is an extension of the work written with Touched Twice clinic coordinators, advocates, professionals, and other volunteers in mind. As I shared this work, people of all ages and life experience found a nugget of truth, a way that they could apply it to their life situations. *The Elijah Project* is Touched Twice for the soul. Are you feeling tired? Is your heart hurting from childhood trauma, disrespect at your job, or disillusionment? Do you feel unappreciated after tirelessly caring for others? This book is designed for you. It was created to be a sanctuary for your soul; a place you can rest, recoup, and recover spiritually.

www.touchedtwiceunited.com

Introduction

God Given Emotions

I was standing in front of a room of men and women who eagerly chatted, smiled, and fidgeted waiting to begin. After a short introduction, I invited the participants to fill out their *Who Am I?* drawings. Adults grabbed at colored pencils and they began drawing, coloring, and enjoying themselves. The room suddenly hushed as I shared my drawing and invited them to share theirs. The first brave table member held up their drawing and began to talk.

I have had the honor of sharing *The Elijah Project* with many groups. Facilitating for people as Elijah's story disarms and invites participants to open up their own journey. As I continued to teach, I felt like the project was more than a onetime program. I believed it was more than a workbook that is finished and set on the shelf to get dusty. I tried to figure out how to make the steps part of an emotional maintenance plan. I tried to figure out how to teach an ongoing process of self-awareness. With mindfulness a hot topic and often misunderstood, I believed there was a Godly way to be aware of our emotional reactions and feeling triggers.

With REST being the result, I wondered if there were five steps that help us circle up. I love alliteration and couldn't help but describe this process with 5 R words. These words have become a mental reminder for how to stand in difficult places, feel difficult emotions and react in a Godly way.

"We shall not cease from exploration,
and the end of all our exploring will be to arrive where
we started and know the place for the first time."
– *T.S. Elliott*

The 5 Rs is a circle because, as T.S. Elliott famously describes, when we tend our emotional garden we will end up at the beginning again. My personal goal for growth is to find myself back at the beginning with more skills, more understanding, and more of the heart of God. The five steps are described below.

REALIZE is the recognition step. It was my *meet my maker moment* highlighted in Chapter 1. Realizing is when your feelings leak out. It's the point at which you bubble over or blow your top. It's the reactive behavior that causes you to kick the dog or yell at fellow drivers on the road. The key is to realize that you are not only angry at the driver; that was just the easy place to express your frustration. There is root to your feeling. In fact, you are not really mad at your dog; it's just an easy target.

REFLECT is the slow down step. After realizing that your reactions are heightened, you just laid on the horn or you took your feelings out on the dog. You STOP. Taking time to reflect is key. This reflection time could be a minute, an hour, or a day. And it is intensely personal. Through *The Elijah Project* we will identify your unique reflection process and incorporate it into a lifestyle of *self-care*.

RECONCILE means to co-exist in harmony. Sometimes it feels like reconciliation is impossible. But it is crucial. Reconciliation comes after you realize the root to the problem and reflect on all the angles of that feeling or situation. Then rather than being a victim to the feelings around the conflict, we identify what can be done to resolve the situation. This step can be summed up this way: *as much as it is up to me.* Sometimes there is a lot we can do and sometimes there is not much we can do to influence a situation. The power of reconciliation is finding a place of resolution within the situation. This can be very difficult in real life situations that extend over time; terminal illness and divorce are examples. The key is to take the philosophy of *as much as it is up to me* into the circumstances and then use all your beautiful *God-care* skills to find the peace of God in the toughest places of life.

REST is the lynch pin of the circle. Often we are drawn to take a nap, pull away, or withdraw before we have done the important step of reconciling. If you take a nap before making the tough phone call, your sleep will be interrupted with dreams and subconscious conflict. The rest step is vitally important for health. *The Elijah Project* defines rest in the context of Elijah's broom tree. It is important to identify what is restful for you. God has designed you unique and special, so rest for your precious soul will look different from another person's rest.

RE-ENGAGE is the final step. When we are hurt, damaged, or exhausted it is imperative to step away, rest, and relax. This is important and as we will learn, the angel gave Elijah time to rest. We have God-given permission to rest. But God has given His people vocation. We are to be His light in a dark world. Therefore we must re-engage with His creation after we have realized, reflected, reconciled, and rested.

The 5 Rs is a simple way to do continuous *God-care*. It is a way to become aware of your body and how certain circumstances affect your emotional balance. God created our bodies to correct themselves. Our bodies respond to stress by moving into the sympathetic nervous system—the part of our physiology designed to keep us alive. It is the part of our chemistry that sends signals to the brain that we may be in danger, commonly understood as *fight, flight, or freeze* response. This automatic response system is very helpful when someone is hurt or when a bear is chasing you. It is not so helpful when a colleague is attacking you in the conference room. When our bodies respond in *fight, flight, or freeze* it moves us away from executive functioning and into survival. God designed us this way. He designed the human body in perfect balance and for it to stay alive. He also gave us beautiful instructions about how to live in His ways while in a broken, survival-oriented world.

> Jesus said: *Peace I leave with you; my peace I give you.*
> *I do not give to you as the world gives.*
> *– John 14:27 NIV*

A peace that surpasses understanding shapes the way we function in a chaotic, drama-fueled culture. So here is how the 5 Rs work: you can close your office door and ask yourself: *Why did I say that like that? I feel anxious, where is that coming from?* or *I feel extremely irritated, why?* This is step one: REALIZE. This step invites us to ask ourselves: *Where am I feeling stress? Are my shoulders tight? Is my heart racing?*

Are my cheeks flushed? And then moves right into step two: REFLECT. This is where we answer the questions listed above: *My face became flushed when my colleague accused me of making a mistake that cost the company a bunch of money. The accusation made me feel incompetent.* Then we can move to step three: RECONCILE. *Is there an immediate step I can take to make this right? Is this problem within my power to resolve? If not, then how can I regain perspective and peace within the situation? Can I take a walk, deep breathe, or put on my favorite worship song?* These actions are part of step four: REST. Make a list of simple *self-care* techniques, like listening to music or lighting a candle. Identify something simple that invites a sense of peace and calms you down so that you can talk with God about how to reconcile the situation. The final step, is step five: RE-ENGAGE. God has called us, His people, to mirror Him in the real world. This means we must continue to work, love, and live in the real world. Once we have received enough perspective about our struggle we must walk back into the office with God's love, grace, and peace, and make it right as much as it is up to us.

Elijah's story serves as a beautiful backdrop to practice *Godly self-care*. Thank you for joining me on the journey.

Chapter 1

Meet My Maker Moment

The morning started out like every other. I woke up and staggered down my awkwardly angled staircase. I let the dog out, pushed start on the coffee pot, and stumbled into the bathroom. I was busily washing my hands when I looked up. Hanging above my double sink was a bevel framed mirror. And inside the mirror, I was greeted by my own haggard reflection. I looked up into the mirror, leaning over the sink. All I could hear in my head was my esthetician friend saying: *As you get older your face falls. Push the lines up.* I pressed my fingers against my wrinkles and smoothed back my crow's feet. Every muscle in my face was stiff. Then in a flash, I thought: *Smile!* So, I smiled at myself. The reflection looking back at me was that of a woman desperately trying to convince someone she was OK. My inner monologue commented: *You are so not OK, Andrea.* My cheeks were stiff and immovable. My mouth curled into a smile but it took pure willpower to keep it that way. It wasn't a natural smile; it was forced and unconvincing, even to me.

I walked away from the mirror and forged into the day. I made lunches, kissed my kids, and waved to the bus. I moved on to do my morning chores. I was a stay-at-home mom and housewife. A few hours later, I was standing in the middle of my tile kitchen floor, when it all came crashing in. As I stood there, I had two haunting thoughts: *I wouldn't want to be married to you,* and *I wouldn't want to be your kid.* I realized what *not being OK* felt like. I had a rush of emotion. *I'm not OK. I'm a therapist; I should know what to do. Do I need counseling? We don't have any money. Is money more important than my health? I need help. I know better than this. I should feel different than this.* It was as if I jumped back and forth between the therapist and client seats. So, if I wasn't crazy before, now I was talking to myself in the middle of my kitchen, questioning whether or not I needed counseling. I think that constitutes a bit of crazy.

Days went by after my kitchen counseling session. I didn't really say anything to anyone. I just felt a deep sense of disappointment, disillusionment, and dissatisfaction growing inside of me. I had spent the first 25 years of my life praying to be a wife and a mother. Now I had it all! I had a great husband, who treated me well and provided for us. I had three beautiful kids, all school age. I lived in rural Middle America in my own house, minus the white picket fence. We had a backyard and a swing set. God had given me everything I had asked for and I felt miserable. This couldn't be right, could it?

The following Sunday I was part of Bible study. We met in our home and were studying *The Story* by Max Lucado and Randy Fraze. The study was good but not rocket science. I was very familiar with the Bible. Having grown up in a pastor's home, gone to Bible college and seminary, and now acting as a pastor's wife, teaching youth group and children's ministry for years, I felt like I knew God's word backwards and forwards. What could be new? We were at the part of the Bible which tells the Prophet Elijah's story. If other group members looked at my face, they might have seen my knowing smile, nod, and dismissal as the story progressed from Elijah telling King Ahab there was going to be a drought to fire coming from heaven on Mount Carmel. And then the rote storytelling stopped. My husband was paraphrasing the story and he said: *After Elijah saw God show up on Mount Carmel and the rain come, Jezebel threatened to end his life. He ran into the desert pouting and complaining.* My husband play acted for Elijah, speaking in an annoying, whiney tone: *I've had enough, let me be with my ancestors.*

I physically jumped! That's me. My balled-up fist was facing heaven saying: *I've had enough. This isn't what I thought it would be. This isn't what I thought it would be like. How could this be it? I've been such a great follower. I deserve better, different. This isn't how it was supposed to be.*

But I can't tell God that I'm so frustrated and I want to quit. Isn't it a sin to tell God that I'm unhappy with my circumstances, when my circumstances aren't that bad? How could I say that to God?

Elijah's story resonated more than I could take in. He came off the greatest high—God sending fire from heaven—and he was plummeted into dismal depression. I too had seen miracles and yet sat frustrated today in my circumstances. The next part of God's story was eye-opening. After ranting to God, Elijah fell asleep under the broom tree. The next thing he knew an angel touched his shoulder and directed him to bread baking on hot coals and a jug of water. The angel said: *Get up and eat.* Elijah ate and drank and then lay down again. Elijah went back to sleep. This was revolutionary to me. Instead of a lightning bolt judging Elijah's frustration, God sent an angel who invited Elijah to eat and drink. Those were His only directions. After eating and drinking, Elijah fell back asleep. Later the angel woke Elijah again and offered him bread and water saying: Get up and eat, for the journey is too much for you. Next the angel directed Elijah to the Mountain of the Lord.

This story was like holy directives from God to me. God sent an angel to take care of Elijah's physical need for food and water and gave him time to go back to sleep. It was like God said: *Andrea, it is OK to take care of yourself.*

I remember leaving Bible study bewildered. An ancient *Old Testament* story told in Sunday school, one that I thought I knew, had actually left me feeling validated and aware of God in a new way. Elijah's story raced through my head. He had been called by God to be a prophet. He had stood up to a wicked king, one who rivaled the *off-with-your-head* Queen of Hearts from *Alice in Wonderland*, and Elijah had been victorious. God had delivered him, and the Israelites had turned back to God acknowledging that He was the King. And then after the miracle—after God delivered His people—Queen Jezebel put a hit out on Elijah's life sending her servant with a message: *If by tonight you are not dead, I will be put to death.* That is quite a bit of collateral. Queen Jezebel laid out her own life in exchange for Elijah's.

Elijah was exhausted. He was hungry and tired. He left his servant behind and ran alone into the wilderness. He ran and ran, a day's journey, before he collapsed under a broom tree. There in a flurry of disappointment and anger, Elijah shook his fist at God and asked Him to take him home. He asked God to let him die so he could be with his family that had gone to be with God. And then Elijah fell asleep. His slumber was disturbed by the touch of an angel. God didn't meet Elijah's cursing threats with a thunderbolt and death. God met Elijah with an angel's touch.

He gave Elijah bread and something to drink and left him. I remember my body melting into the story. The angel simply asked him to take care of his body and left him to sleep. I love to sleep. I am intimately aware of the soft, nurturing comfort of my bed. And I would welcome more time resting. God gave Elijah permission to rest.

It was after this part of Elijah's journey that I was pressed to go back and visit how he got there. How had his journey begun and what more could I glean from it?

Stephen Covey encourages in *7 Habits of Highly Effective People* to begin with the end in mind. With a firm vision of the end of the story, I went back to the beginning and walked with Elijah from his call to its completion.

Now Elijah the Tishbite, from Tishbe in Gilead, said to Ahab, "As the Lord, the God of Israel, lives, whom I serve, there will be neither dew nor rain in the next few years except at my word."
– *1 Kings 17:1 NIV*

Elijah's name means *Yahweh is God*. He is a Tishbite herdsman from Gilead. Tishbe is a place that no longer appears on a map today. So Elijah, a hearty man who worked the land from an insignificant town that no longer exists, was directed by God to go tell the king of Samaria (the southern kingdom of Israel) that there was going to be a drought. He had a message that was unattractive and bad for the community and he went to tell King Ahab that misfortune and trial were coming to his kingdom.

Wherever Elijah traveled his name announced to everyone the God he served. Elijah was a God-fearer living within a divided kingdom. The Israelites were led by kings who worshipped many gods. The people had many idols which pushed out the one true God. Elijah defended the worship of God. Elijah was directed by God to give King Ahab a message: A drought was coming. Immediately after Elijah delivered the message, God directed him to the Kerith Valley where he was fed morning and evening by ravens.

The therapist in me stopped at verse one. The verse sent me reeling back to my tile kitchen floor and the thought: *I am not the kind of mother or wife that I dreamed of being.* I asked the question: *Who am I?* then began to imagine what I looked like inside and out. Another part of me, the therapist, was yearning to ask the hard feeling questions: *Why did I feel anxious? What was causing my anxiety? What was causing the feelings of discontentment? Why when I had a good marriage, healthy children, and even a beautiful dog was I feeling so disillusioned?* So, I invited God to do therapy on me. I grabbed a piece of paper and some colored pencils and drew a squiggly outline of a person. My person had hunched shoulders and eyes that faced the ground. It depicted a heart bursting out of my chest and swirls in my stomach. I felt anxious and nauseous.

If I was a better artist I would have covered myself up … because I felt like hiding. This is an example of my *Who am I?* drawing.

Realizing was the first step. I took some time to think about how I felt. I scanned my body head to toe evaluating where I was holding stress, what was feeling good, and analyzing what I might be avoiding. The next part of the realization process was to take a step backwards. Elijah understood what his name meant. His name meant: *Yahweh is God.* He had a clear vision and calling on his life. Everywhere Elijah went from the time he was a little boy, people knew he was a God-follower. This introduction gives us a framework to put Elijah's present task in context to his past experience. So, step two of my self-therapy was to ask myself: *Andrea how did you get here?* That led me to squiggle a line across a piece of paper. I wrote on the right end of the line "THIS IS ME" and then worked backwards to try to identify what was going on in my journey. It led me back to where I was stuck.

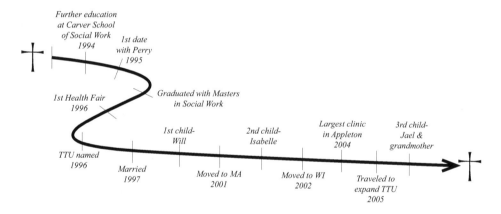

Andrea's Timeline

As I began to write my story using images and color, I realized a few more things about myself. Sometime over the past year I had stopped answering my phone. I let calls automatically go to voicemail. It was a self-protective mechanism intended to keep me safe from critical voices. My role as a pastor's wife had become overwhelming. I had ceased to worship on Sunday morning overcome by the heat of our parishioners' stares. It was like they were boring a hole in my head, exposing my deepest insecurities. I stopped looking people in the eyes. I felt afraid. I felt exposed.

At this time I was leading a group of preschool moms who met weekly to study the Bible and pray for each other. I brought all my new found insight to the group. I looked up and against my better judgment I said: *I'm not OK, I'm not sure I can make it as your pastor's wife. I'm not the woman I dreamed of being. I prayed for the first 25 years of my life that I would find a godly husband. I got him and we are in ministry together and all I want to do is quit. I want to give my husband back. I prayed and prayed to be a mom and at the moment, I'm not liking it. I want to give the kids back too. No one has cancer. No one has died. My house is still standing and yet, I want to cash in on a return policy. I can't take care of them if I can't take care of me. I don't know how to do both!*

The women greeted me with love and grace. My vivacious, eccentric friend who always came to group dressed to the nines was wearing a white and black rabbit skin coat and spiky heals. She looked at me and said: *I can't believe you feel this way. What do we do?*

My vulnerability slipped back into guidance and I suggested that we do the Henry Cloud, John Townsend *Boundaries* study together. The women looked around the table with no better ideas and agreed: *Anything to help.* Little did we know that the 22 week study would take us months and months to complete. When the directives would get too hard we would set the book aside and take a break. For me the *Boundaries* study opened my eyes to so many places where I was stuck. It helped me realize that I was waiting for other people to take care of me, watch out for me, and protect me. My innocence was leaving me unprotected and exposed. This was not only emotionally unhealthy, it was biblically inaccurate.

Equipped with new skills from *Boundaries*, I began to experience Elijah's story in 3D. Elijah the prophet a Tishbite from Tishbe; Andrea living in Middle America, the little town of Chippewa Falls. Elijah the herdsman; Andrea the wife, mother and lifelong Christ-follower.

Details in my history revealed new parts of my destiny. It was during this season that I distinctly remember standing in the mid-section of the movie theater where our church met, preparing to teach a Sunday school class. Armed with my Bible and photocopied worksheets, I looked up into the empty stadium-style seating. I had hurriedly gotten my kids ready that morning. I had quickly applied a little makeup. And standing there

I questioned: *What was the rush for? There might be five to ten people present today. Why was I working so hard and preparing so diligently?* Vain thoughts entered again: *I don't think this church realizes how talented I am. I could be speaking to hundreds of people right now.* Not really! Yet the raw explosion of pride was met by the soft whisper of God. I have never really heard the voice of God. I've never had the silence broken by a Morgan Freeman type narration, but I have often experienced the unshakable, unavoidable presence of God in my being. He has told me what to do. He has answered my prayers with a thought or an insight. He has been alive. This morning He said: *Andrea whether it is for five or five thousand, do it unto Me.*

Ouch, that smarts. I felt it more than words on my ears, more like a quake in my soul. It was a deep knowing that I could not avoid. And every time I grumbled about preparing lessons for 20 teenagers or watching babies in the nursery, His words rose up deep from within my soul: *Do it for Me.*

So Elijah a prophet of God from Tishbe in Gilead, told King Ahab there was going to be a drought. That is it that is how it began! The story from more than 2000 years ago met mine and started me on a journey of self-understanding and *God-care* for my soul. God radically changed the way I did therapy. He asked me to tell His story and promised it would bring healing into others' stories. He began to revolutionize the way I viewed the *Old Testament*. No longer were these Scriptures old impertinent stories, instead the stories came alive. And I had so much more in common with the characters than I had ever imagined.

Andrea is a Christ-follower from the age of four, raised in Massachusetts, educated at Gordon College and Southern Baptist Theological seminary, pastor's wife and stay-at-home mother of three, temporarily retired licensed clinical social worker, called by God to use all her skills, knowledge, and ability to understand Him better and share the story with everyone she could.

Provision to Ponder

What is on your mind and heart today? Where do you feel happy, loved, and cared for? Where are you holding your stress, anxiety, or frustration?

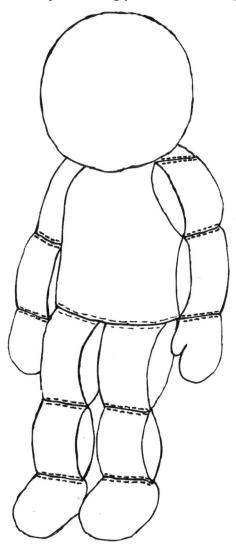

Chapter 2

Where God Guides He Will Provide

My husband first saw our house on-line. It was a tiny thumbnail photo. When we arrived to take a look it was a mere shell. It was abandoned, empty, and old. The back window was broken, so we climbed inside to walk around. I had asked God for two things before we went house shopping: a backyard and a big window to see the backyard from the kitchen. We walked through the house laughing because it reminded us of *The Brady Bunch* house. The powder blue carpet, dark wood paneling, and gold curtains took me right back to childhood. We walked from room to room laughing and joking until we reached the kitchen. I stopped short, and gasped. There before me was a glass patio door framing a picture perfect backyard. My mind traveled from the past and charged into the future imagining my children's squeals as they played on the swing set, ran with the dog, and climbed the trees.

For our first year on County Highway S we reclaimed space room by room. Our son slept on his mattress in the living room, our daughter's pack-n-play was in the laundry room, and my husband and I stayed in the downstairs bedroom. We worked to claim the un-redeemable upstairs space. We found out years later that the upstairs had been home to 11 children during the heyday of the home. We discovered an old David Cassidy poster and a large black grate where the heat would pump upstairs. The appraiser was unwilling to survey the upstairs, calling it unlivable space. We built walls, painted, and carpeted the upstairs. This home became a safe place for our family and more. This home is where our children have grown and thrived, and it has been a safe space for many in our church community. We have hosted small groups, cookouts, and youth group.

This was the fifth house I lived in during the course of my life. And I've lived in it for 15 years. My timeline highlights the starts and stops on my journey. The timeline is a snapshot of my journey, just looking at God's provision. Above the timeline demarks when we had plenty and below the timeline demarks when we didn't. I put a cross at the beginning and at the end because He has been with us the entire time. But sometimes were definitely harder than others.

My timeline is a snapshot of my story. As the years go by it is easy to chalk things up to been there, done that, but when I pull out my timeline and truly reflect on the good times and the bad, I am amazed by how God used specific experiences—things that just seemed like needless suffering—to prepare me for the next part of my journey. This is my timeline reflecting on God's provision.

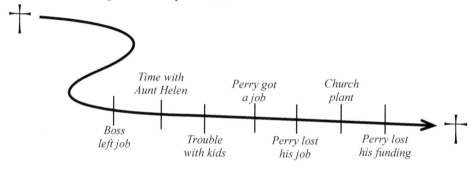

Then the word of the Lord came to Elijah: "Leave here, turn eastward and hide in the Kerith Ravine, east of the Jordan. You will drink from the brook, and I have directed the ravens to supply you with food there."
– 1 Kings 17:2-4 NIV

Elijah boldly told King Ahab that a drought was coming. God in turn directed Elijah away from danger and impending death to the Kerith Ravine. This was a rugged place, a hilly desolate wilderness. No doubt, King Ahab immediately sent troops looking for Elijah. God's cleft in the rock saved Elijah from the soldiers' purview.

History tells us that Elijah spent most of the three-year drought in the Kerith Ravine. This is a long time to be isolated from community and dependent on the daily provision of God. This was a tough calling, yet necessary for his survival. My childhood memory conjures up a Sunday school image of Elijah like an elegant painting hanging in a famous art museum. He is sprawled out on a rock, his cloaks billowing in the wind as a giant bird drops finger sandwiches into his mouth. Elijah's eyes are upturned to heaven and his mouth is curled into a gentle, satisfied smile.

My childhood interpretation was transformed when I realized that the giant birds are ravens: huge, black, dirty scavengers. They search the scourged wilderness landscape for road kill. This is the meat they brought Elijah. It was sun dried road kill, not tuna fish finger sandwiches.

I have taken a few rugged camping trips in my life. Not many— because as I have grown older I appreciate down comforters and temperature controlled rooms. But when I was young and trying to impress a young man, I went on a camping trip that required a thing called a bear bag. Right after our campfire dinner we would seal up our food, wrap it in a canvas tarp, and string it up high in a tree. I never saw a bear and I always had food for one more meal.

Elijah was given just enough provision for his physical needs. The ravens brought bread and meat every morning and evening. The provisions were perfect proportions. There was just enough food for each meal and there was nothing left over. This didn't just serve God's master plan for dependence on Him; it also provided safety for Elijah. Since there was no food left over, there was no worry of wild animals rooting around his camp at night.

These birds deposited perfectly portioned scraps for Elijah each morning and evening. They in fact were the embodiment of Jesus' *New Testament* teaching in the Lord's Prayer: *give us today our daily bread*. Eugene Peterson quotes Jesus saying: *Keep us alive with three square meals*. This is daily provision. It is both countercultural and difficult. I like fluffy homemade bread in ample supply, preserved in gallon size zip-style bags, and kept in the refrigerator. I like my pantry to offer a variety of options for dinner. I am like most Americans with enough food stored in my cupboard and my freezer to keep my family fed for a month without ration.

I like the concept of daily bread but I despise its application. I like to know that I will be taken care of tomorrow, and the next day, and the day after that. I don't just want to know I will be provided for; I want to know what God will provide for me. Everything around me feeds into my thinking. Even the idea of saving for a rainy day gives me a false sense of security. I find myself trusting my own savings account rather than God's provision.

The Bible only tells us so much. It reports that Elijah was led to the Kerith Ravine. It recounts that ravens brought him breakfast and dinner. It says that Elijah drank from the brook and Elijah lived in this wilderness location for more than two years, but not more than three. God's word doesn't say that Elijah built a house. It doesn't say that Elijah had neighbors. It doesn't say that Elijah created a community. Actually all historical accounts point to solitary years, a time when Elijah connected with God alone.

Below is a snapshot of Elijah's journey during this period of time. The highlights are above the line and the lowlights are below. Like my journey, the one consistent force throughout the timeline is God.

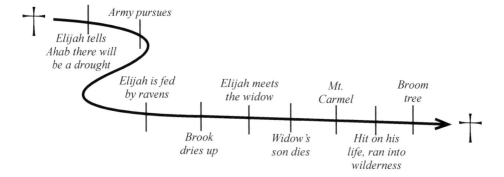

It can be easy to put Elijah and his story in a box, labeled *a long time ago* and leave it there as an interesting historical reference. This is a two year portion of Elijah's real story. It isn't the beginning of his walk with God or the end, but it is significant. No matter where you find yourself on the journey today it is significant.

Provision to Ponder

Using colors, symbols, and words share your story. Move backwards from today to a place where you have felt stuck. Use a red pencil, pen, or marker and circle the places of struggle. Use a green pencil, pen, or marker to circle the places where you see growth.

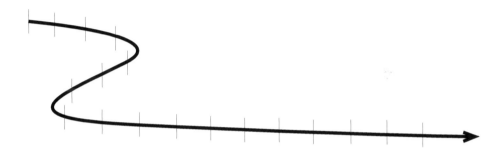

> Where do you still feel stuck?
> Is there an action step you can take to get unstuck?

Now, take a few moments to fill in the timeline below with your own provision story. First remember the times of plenty and fill them in above the line. Then remember the times of want and fill them in below the line. Finally go back through the timeline and add a cross to signify God's presence in your journey. If God was not a part of your life at that time but He is now, reflect on where God might have been even if you didn't recognize Him.

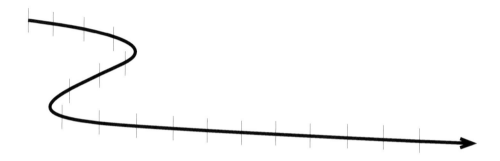

🕊 Reflect on God's miraculous provision.

🕊 Where do you need some provision today?

The Power of the Lord's prayer

> **Our Father who art in Heaven**
> **hallowed be thy name.**
> **Thy kingdom come, thy will be done,**
> **on earth as it is in Heaven.**
> **Give us this day our daily bread**
> **and forgive us our trespasses,**
> **as we forgive those who trespass against us.**
> **Lead us not into temptation**
> **but deliver us from evil.**
> **For thine is the kingdom, the power**
> **and the glory, for ever and ever.**
> **Amen**

Rewrite the Lord's prayer in your own words

Reflect on God's daily bread

Consider the list of people who have sinned against you. What does a step toward forgiveness look like?

Chapter 3

The Brook Dries Up

Some time later the brook dried up because there had been no rain in the land. Then the word of the Lord came to him: "Go at once to Zarephath in the region of Sidon and stay there."
– 1 Kings 17:7-9 NIV

Growing up in New England when I would complain about the weather, someone would say: *Wait a minute*. The weather could literally change in an instant. Life is similar. There are no guarantees, but a few things are for sure. Things will change. Our kids will grow up. King Solomon lamented about the seasons of life. Seasons will change. In Ecclesiastes he suggests activities that are connected to those seasons like life and death.

Following God is not a spectator sport. This was the tagline for our church while we studied the book of *Acts*. It sticks in my mind because it rings true. It seems that as soon as I become comfortable with the world around me, something changes. Sometimes I become comfortable with how uncomfortable I am, and don't want to change that either. I would prefer to sit in my messed up sand box brewing over betrayal or worrying over what ifs. But, stewing leads to stagnation. And Satan loves stagnation. I can see him rubbing his hands with delight, rejoicing over my being stuck.

Following God is not a spectator sport. It is a full-contact, down-and-dirty mission to bring His light into a dark world. When God spoke, Elijah listened and obeyed. The divine voice of God told him that a drought was coming to the kingdom of Samaria. Elijah prophesied to King Ahab about the three-year calamity that was to come. After Elijah prophesied, God directed him to the Kerith Valley where ravens fed him bread and meat every morning and evening. Elijah drank from a brook. God protected Elijah by providing for him. The ravens' portions were perfect provision and Elijah had nothing left over, protecting him from wild animals scouring for food.

I can barely imagine myself in the place of Elijah, reaching up to God trusting that He would literally shower me with provisions from the sky. The image that comes to mind is me, clinging to my computer keyboard, a file folder, or meeting notes, believing that these will link me to God's provision and missing the much more ample supply. Depending upon the moment you might catch one paper-cut hand half reaching to the sky, while the other hand works hard to provide for itself. I suppose that over the years there was comfort in the predictability of God's provision for Elijah. There was a satisfaction in the structure around the faith that Elijah modeled. I spend a lot of time managing, organizing, and rearranging deck chairs in my life. God invites us to fellowship with Him. He wants us to hang out and allow Him to provide. He isn't as interested in my control.

Following the God of Abraham, Isaac, and Jacob is counter-cultural to the Western way of life. It is easy to put ourselves in the place of the provider. We confuse the lavish gifts that God bestows on us with rewards for our hard work. We take the provisions and view them as deserved residual for our own work. It is integral to biblical living to understand all good and perfect gifts flow from the Father of Heavenly Lights.

The consequence of Adam and Eve's choice to compete with God's supremacy was an end—an end to paradise, an end to unhindered communion with God, and end to a perfect connection with each other. The fall initiated death. Loss is a consequence of the curse. Creation's perfection was broken after the serpent successfully deceived Eve. God cursed the earth and in that moment humans began to toil, feel pain, and experience death. Before the fall there was no life cycle, which I believe is a vision of the future. God designed perpetual life, different from the cycle of life we live with today. In the book of *Revelation*, John shares a dream of God's future. He describes trees which always bear fruit. The natural human inclination is to not want to say goodbye. The human yearning for everlasting life is God-wired. The human desire to move away from pain and loss is part of the divine spark. Everlasting life is what we were made for. It is part of being made in the image of God.

Alas, we live in the shadow of the fall. And God has provided us the emotion of grief to allow us to process loss. Grief is the sorrowful feeling that accompanies the death of someone or something. American culture supports striving, pushing through, and making things happen. This does not leave much room for grief. The idea of pausing to acknowledge endings is healthy. The end of a job, graduation from school, moving, changing churches, finishing projects, saying goodbye to a friend after a visit or forever as a result of death, are all found on the continuum of endings.

Humans rebel against loss. Loss and change can bring both positive and negative stress. Researchers Holmes and Rahe created an empirically valid stress scale. It provides a list of life events. The scale gives numeric value to the stressful events in our lives occurring over a one year period of time. The tool lists both positive and negative stressors—marriage, moving, a job change, death of a loved one. This stress is part of the consequence of the fall. God told Adam and Eve when they were leaving the garden that now life would be hard, there would be work. God knew He had hard-wired us for life. The struggle with death is a result of the curse.

Life outside the Garden of Eden is full of necessary endings. Years ago I decided I was going to plant my own vegetable garden. I borrowed a friend's rototiller. After unsuccessfully operating it, I coaxed my husband into tilling the land. I planted my seeds. And for three weeks, I weeded and watered it. Then we went on vacation. We were gone for two weeks. When I got back my small plot of earth was overgrown. I looked at the mess and thought: *I'll buy my carrots at the grocery store.* I never dreamed of having my own garden again. This reminds me of some great advice I received in college. My professor Sybil Coleman said: *Life is like a garden. You start on one end and weed your way across just to find that by the time you get to the end, the weeds are poking though the area you started in.* We tend the soil of our lives, plant new adventures, water the ground of hardship and care for it as best we can, but death comes. It robs us of the life we dreamed of regarding our job, our marriage, our loved ones, or our friendships. Death reaches us and things end.

Dr. Henry Cloud in his book *Necessary Endings* suggests that our relationships are like a rose bush. When you prune a rose bush, taking away good buds as well as bad, the roses end up healthier, bigger, and stronger. We need to prune our relationships, cutting back connections that are injurious or dead in order to be available for new relationship life.

Over the history of my life quite a few of my friendships have dried up. The first time it happened, I fought very hard to keep the relationship going. I questioned what I was doing wrong. I wondered how I could rekindle the friendship that had once meant so much. It is easier to talk about the relationship that quietly fades—not from lack of care but because of lack of proximity, common interest, or time. The relationships that changed because I moved or my friend moved could be chalked up to natural circumstance. The relationships that are more difficult to talk about are the ones that actually became unhealthy. More than once I have woken up to the reality that a friend was actually not an ally. Whether intentional or not, the friend had stopped supporting me to be the best me. In fact, the relationship was tearing me down inside and out. The relationship had become toxic. One day I took notice of what my friend was saying. The little comments that were eating away my other relationships, and the negative comments about my husband and criticism of my children.

As we look at Elijah's story we see just that. God brought people, places, and activities into Elijah's life for a season. God asked him to be faithful to the task of prophesy where he was, and in relationship when appropriate, and then God led him on his next mission. Elijah watched his daily provisions change. As the drought progressed, his surroundings became more desolate. The ground became more degraded. As the days moved to weeks, and months turned into years, the ground lay fallow. The animals were starving. The wild animals withered and there was no meat on their bones. The ravens' daily provisions were now mere remnants of the meat that they had once provided. The birds were picking off the bones of emaciated road kill. If Elijah had stayed in the Kerith Ravine, he would surely die.

The Bible gives us a clear picture through the story of Elijah of one way to handle endings. When the brook dried up, Elijah moved on. Too often I am the woman digging deeper in the dried, parched earth to find water. I move further up the stream in hopes of finding something alive. Elijah's story is a beautiful reminder that God as my Protector and Provider will continue to be with me wherever I go. He will give me what I need. He will provide. I don't need to prop things up and frustrate the dry earth to find water, I need to trust that when I follow His directions the next provision will be there.

Before we move on in Elijah's story, we must stop and reflect on our own losses. We must grieve what and who we have lost. We must acknowledge that loss is difficult and that our very human nature fights against accepting it.

My house is a ranch style home spread out over ¾ acres. It's the last house on the left side of our street in desperate need of a paint job. At a time when we needed provision, a parishioner offered to paint it. That alone was a fantastic gift. Not only did they offer to paint, but they did some much needed repair to the exterior. The demolition revealed significant squirrel damage. A mother squirrel had scratched and clawed and tried to dig her way deep into the side of our house. While removing rotten wood, the workman discovered a nest with eight newborn squirrels.

The work uncovered that the second floor window casings had rotted out and there were large holes exposing the interior of the house to the elements. The original offer to paint our house became a blessing ten times over as the repairs served to winterize our home.

God provided for us through the gift of the workman. But, the repairs for us represented a loss for the mother squirrel.

The mother squirrel who took up residence in our home wasn't trying to be a menace. She was attempting to protect her babies from danger. She had worked hard to burrow deeper and deeper into our siding so that her offspring had a chance for survival. The mother squirrel didn't know this was the year we would receive a gift and have the exterior of our house repaired. She didn't know that her hard work to cover up would be uncovered so quickly by the workman's crowbar. She didn't know her fate was about to change anymore that I knew how Elijah's journey with God would alter the way I did life.

Provision to Ponder

I encourage you to download Holmes and Rahe stress scale: *www.stress.org/holmes-rahe-stress-inventory/* Take time to reflect on the past year of your personal journey. This tool may give words for your broken heart as you reflect on all of the good and bad experiences you have had over the past 12 months.

King Solomon left a wonderful passage of scripture that puts endings in the context of everyday life. May you find comfort in his famous words.

> **There is a time for everything and a season for every activity under the heavens;**
> a time to be born and a time to die,
> a time to plant and a time to uproot,
> a time to kill and a time to heal,
> a time to tear down and a time to build,
> a time to weep and a time to laugh,
> a time to mourn and a time to dance,
> a time to scatter stones and a time to gather them,
> a time to embrace and a time to refrain from embracing,
> a time to search and a time to give up,
> a time to keep and a time to throw away,
> a time to tear and a time to mend,
> a time to be silent and a time to speak,
> a time to love and a time to hate,
> a time to war and a time for peace.
> *– Ecclesiastes 3:1-8 NIV*

Review the list of activities in *Ecclesiastes*. Identify what *season* or *time* you are in now? What do you need to end, so you can celebrate the next season? Use the trees on the previous page to mark those seasons.

🕊 Take a look at your life, as Dr. Cloud suggests, what needs to be pruned?

🕊 Review the list of activities in *Ecclesiastes.*

🕊 What is *your time* now?

🕊 What needs to end to celebrate *your time*?

🕊 Start with a simple step: consider your possessions.

🕊 What is it time to keep?

🕊 What is it time to throw away?

Repeat these questions for: responsibilities, activities, relationships, and dreams.

Chapter 4

Safe People: Are There Any?

I was invited to speak for a ladies' luncheon at Byfield Parish Church in Massachusetts, the church where I grew up. I accepted the invitation with fear and trembling. I knew my Sunday school teachers, youth group leader, and choir director would all be present to listen. In my head I thought that they were coming to evaluate how well they had taught me. I imagined they were there to scrutinize my scripture memory, how I handled the biblical text, and my understanding of the overall message of the Bible. I had all but convinced myself that the luncheon attendees were my enemies. My inner monologue condemned me before I opened my mouth. I had prepared my opening remarks to highlight that feeling of discernment and vulnerability. I shared with some friends before I left my Midwestern home, that I hoped this opportunity would help me deal with a "stuck" place in my heart. I knew I must face head-on the truth of my past, in order to heal.

The truth of my past was that I was desperately afraid of *not being good enough.* As a child my personality translated encouragement to pressure and caused me to constantly strive to be better and better. When I went to Seminary I remember telling my Mom that I was going to go easy on myself. I was going to enjoy learning and just relax. She came to visit me in Louisville and while taking a walk one beautiful warm night, I will never forget her saying: *Andrea, you have straight A's. I thought you were going to take it easy.* This sums up how I did my life. I was an overachiever. There was no taking it easy. Whatever I did, I did with two hundred percent of my effort. As a pastor's wife, people felt comfortable and at ease with me and many times that gave rise to a sort of open season of sharing. Parishioners would feel free to share all that they were disappointed in about our church, my husband and ultimately - me. The truth of my past was actually the truth of my present. I was desperately afraid that my best, no matter how hard I worked, prepared, or perfected, would not be good enough. That fear was reinforced with each morsel of constructive criticism. I felt deep in my being that my good wasn't good enough and that was where I was stuck.

Remember *Molasses Swamp* in the classic game *Candyland*? Satan, the father of lies, had me stuck in molasses. It was icky sticky black goo stuck to my legs and feet trapping me. Satan is not privy to the future, he only knows our past. So he takes the past and invades our present with memories and thoughts of regret. He convinces us of two lies: first that God isn't enough, and second that we are better off without God and others. He strikes fear in our hearts and uses that fear to isolate us from God and community. He enslaves us in darkness.

My dreams were doomed before I began because my life experience (the part Satan was wielding) told me: *everything I said, everything I did or did not do would be used against me at some time. My mistakes and errors in judgment whether made by accident or on purpose would be listed in permanent ink on a huge billboard. That was how it had always been and that is how it would always be.* It was easier to stay home, cuddle up under the covers, watch hours of *Gilmore Girls* on DVD, and not answer my phone. Satan replayed the nasty comments and disparaging observations over and over again. I had two choices: to stay in bed secluded from friends and relationships, or I could take everything I knew of who God was and is and will be and step out with faith into the scary world with God.

The luncheon day arrived. Moments before I was to take the stage and begin teaching, I ran into a childhood friend's mother. We chatted about life which had dealt her heavy losses including the death of her husband. As we talked about her loss and shared stories from the past, I began to feel disarmed. My defenses came down and I was reminded again of all God had provided for me. When the conversation turned toward me, she asked how I was doing. I told her the truth. I was nervous and intimidated by this speaking engagement. She patiently looked at me and said: *Andrea we are your fans.* It was an amazing pendulum swing. Suddenly, I felt the weight I was carrying fall from my shoulders. I stood up taller and breathed a little deeper. The pit in my stomach dissipated and I felt free. What an awesome feeling to reframe the audience from critics to fans!

> **"Don't be afraid. Go home and do as you have said.**
> **But first make a small loaf of bread for me …"**
> *— 1 King 17:10 NIV*

The widow in Elijah's story is stuck with an identity based on her social situation. She is now a widow, a woman with no husband, a woman without social status. She is a woman without a name: simply called, *widow*. In ancient times a widow was a person *not chosen*. It is difficult to grasp the enormity of this woman's plight. In our society women live with freedom to be educated, single, and independent. But this woman, this widow was scorned. In ancient times, a woman was first a daughter, then given to her husband like property, then she hoped and prayed to be a mother of sons. One of these three men kept her securely attached within society. The son was the last strand of hope in case her father and husband died. She was defined by the men in her life. This woman had absolutely no value apart from her role as wife and mother. I am a woman living in the West defined by the expectations of my role as pastor's wife.

I have felt the power of whispers and the weight of penetrating stares. Although we are separated by 20 generations and thousands of miles, I understand the widow. When we break into her story, she is gathering sticks at a time of day sanctioned by the government. During this time in history, the outcasts were permitted to visit the city square during the heat of the day when the other community members were enjoying the cool of their homes. The unlovely were relegated to do their public chores at the most difficult part of the day. This day started out like any other, she was a woman called widow.

Elijah's map led him to Zarephath. He stood outside of the city gate and called to the widow. I wonder if she looked over her shoulder, thinking Elijah was addressing someone else. Remarkably, she answered him. Elijah asked for a cup of water and then asked for a cake of bread. The widow responded to Elijah in the vulnerability of her reality. She said: *I am gathering sticks to make a fire, to make my last loaf of bread before my son and I will die*. Elijah is audacious with his request. He asked the widow, a marginalized woman, who has nothing, in the midst of a drought, to give him food and water. The widow tells the truth, exposing

35

her limitations. She says: *I have nothing to give.* And Elijah asks her to give the little she has anyway. And she gives what she can.

When he came to the town gate, a widow was there gathering sticks.
– 1 King 17:10-13 NIV

When I was a teenager, I got my first set of contact lenses. They were gas permeable which was a hybrid between hard and soft lenses. The first weekend I wore the contacts my eyes burned, itched, and left my eyes red. I constantly felt like I had something in my eye. They were uncomfortable when I had them in, but I couldn't see when I had them out. Gas permeable lens are rigid. My eyes didn't like them and wanted to push them out. The brilliant design took my tears, the very signal that something foreign was invading my eye, to fill the gap between the piece of plastic and my pupil. The tears became a cushion so my eye would accept the corrective lens. Gas permeable lens re-contour the eye. In fact, after three years of wearing these lenses, my astigmatism changed and I no longer needed contacts at all.

Elijah met the widow at the city gate. Let's imagine the city gate like my contact lens. It is designed to provide protection for its inhabitants. Elijah stood outside the city gate and called in. The widow answered, brought him food, and let him in. The Bible distinctly states that God prepared the widow: "Go at once to Zarephath in the region of Sidon and stay there. I have directed a widow to supply you with food." Just as God instructed Elijah where to go and who to talk to, God spoke to the widow and guided her to invite Elijah in. God is the best director to help us open and close the gates to our hearts. Dr. Cloud and Dr. Townsend teach that boundaries are like a picket fence with a gate. This is not a brick wall, a structure where we can't see out and others can't see in. Rather it is a wood fence, with slats, that protects us from intruders. We can see out and others can peer in. The gate is powered by us. We open and shut the gate as we see fit.

Boundaries are tricky. I personally prefer a wall to a fence. Walls are solid. They start and stop and I feel safe when the wall is up. It's like putting a fortress around my heart to keep me safe. When I have my wall up, I am insulated and protected from attacks. I feel invincible. When my wall is up, I am also distant and alone. When my wall is down, my heart is soft; I share about my struggles and I present myself vulnerably. I feel most myself with my wall down, but this is also when I often feel most victimized. The concrete wall, while providing protection, is an unhealthy boundary. It might protect me, but it also separates me.

Healthy boundaries are like gas permeable contact lenses. When you haven't had boundaries they feel foreign. You want to take the contacts out. You want to take the fence down. You want to swing open the gate. Or you want to reassemble the wall. Brick by brick it feels better to have that solid boundary. At the first bit of resistance from a friend or family member who wants you to bend to their will, you want to protect yourself by pushing them out or acquiesce by pleasing them. I remember wearing my contacts for the first time on Sunday morning. I counted down the minutes until Sunday school and church were over so I could go home, take them out, and put my glasses back on. Just as my eyes had to become accustomed to contact lenses, practicing boundaries is an art that must be exercised. There is a time for opening the gate and letting people in, and there is a time to close the gate and watch from the other side. Just because someone wants to be close to me, doesn't mean they have earned the right to hear my precious stories. I have learned the hard way that sharing honestly and openly about my family or my marriage can leave a lot of collateral damage. Exercising healthy boundaries doesn't only support me, it protects my loved ones from the wolf in sheep's clothing.

Once I had a blown glass heart necklace. I liked to wear it because it reminded me of my vulnerability. The glass pendant represented my propensity to hurt and be hurt. Whenever I would wear it, my fingers would caress the bulb and it would help me relax. Sometimes I felt like I was massaging my own heart when I touched it. I would long for someone to take my heart and hold it, treasure it, and keep it safe. The risk in earthly relationships is that my heart is never really safe. Sometimes people say things that are hurtful. Sometimes people are insensitive, or worse— sometimes people have used my vulnerability to make themselves feel better.

A few years ago I was getting dressed for a date night with my husband. I grabbed my blown glass heart necklace off the bathroom sink. The black cord slipped through my fingers and as I reached out in desperation to save it, the glass heart struck the unforgiving ceramic tile and shattered. The red glass lay crushed in a pile of debris on the floor. That pile of glass rubble is an image for what it feels like to be betrayed in relationship.

I had a friend who enjoyed a lot of the same things I did. We spent a lot of time together. I thought our friendship was doing well and that everything was going along great. One day I received an old-school letter in the mail. The letter was handwritten and began innocuously, but ended with a list of ways I had disappointed her. It felt like a gut punch. *How could I have missed the signs? Why didn't she tell me in person?*

This type of thing has happened many times over different contexts throughout my life. I developed a variety of ways of coping with the feeling of betrayal. Sometimes I pulled the covers up over my head and stayed in bed. Sometimes I acted ungodly by ranting to another friend about the reasons I was right and the person who hurt me was wrong. And still other times, I practiced calculated control by acting in a counselor role, distancing myself emotionally. I listened and reflected, but didn't share deeply or vulnerably.

Two of my reactions were really connected. The counselor role put me in an untouchable category. I was a trained listener and I was good at it. I could easily use up my friendship time by listening and reflecting, never needing to share myself. This tactic kept me emotionally insulated and protected from the pain of betrayal. This also left me walled off, stuck and isolated in my own pain. It left me lonely and with a powder keg of emotion, so the next unsuspecting person, safe or not, would receive an explosion of my feelings.

The other familiar coping mechanism came in the form of gossip and slander. I would rather use different, less sin-revealing language—words like processing or telling the truth, but if I call it what it is, I had actually learned from an early age that the best way to feel better about myself was to make someone else feel small. If I listened well enough, unearthed the other person's flaws, I could exploit their weaknesses by sharing their faults with others behind their back. Of course it was all OK, because I couched it as a prayer request or heart-felt Godly concern. This made me feel much better for a moment. But when I got off the phone or walked away from the conversation, I had a sense of paranoia. I knew I had violated trust and acted less than virtuously. It made me wonder for weeks: *did the victim of my words know what I had said? When was it all going to come back and haunt me?*

Reflecting on this behavioral pattern revealed a huge area where I needed to grow. The widow's story became a mirror, revealing God's way to handle overwhelming life situations. Her story pressed me to trust God even when it seemed ridiculous. It took practice to walk away from disparaging conversations or better yet to actually stop them. It was during my quest to find a safe person that I realized I was looking for something I was not. This struggle forced me to come face-to-face with my reflection in the mirror. I wanted other people to be something I wasn't brave enough to be myself.

> **"The jar of flour will not be used up and the jug of oil will not run dry until the day of the Lord sends rain on the land."**
> **– *1 Kings 17:14 NIV***

And the widow does as Elijah requested. Our story continues with Elijah living with the widow and her son. It is a marvel to imagine God's unique provision. In a culture where we have IRAs and other investments for our future, the widow had jars of flour and oil. Every time she made a loaf of bread her cup hit the bottom of the empty jug. She literally scraped the bottom of the barrel. She would dip her scoop, and miraculously there was just enough for her to make another loaf of bread. The drought was all around them. The widow's household was provided for every day while other families were not. And the next day, when it was time to bake, the widow opened her cupboard and had just enough, one scoop of flour, one tablespoon of oil, and she made another loaf of bread.

Physical provision is very important to me. I have known the feeling of scarcity: the reality that the checkbook is overdrawn and the mortgage payment is due the next day. And I know scarcity in the form of emotional depletion, the feeling that you can't dig any deeper and that the creek has dried up. I teach youth group. Every Wednesday night a gaggle of teens bounds off the school bus and piles into my home. A small band of volunteers and I prepare and serve dinner, lead games, and teach teens in our neighborhood from the Bible. Teens are like little whirlwinds. Their emotions are a tangle while they drop belongings, wrappers, and other sorts of items on my living room floor and beyond. Many Wednesday mornings, I wake up tired and think: *I would rather get a pedicure tonight. I wish someone would come to clean my house instead of watching my house be torn up.* There are many Wednesday mornings when I question why God has me doing this ministry. I cry out with resentment. It is on these worst Wednesday mornings, when my thoughts are most sinister, and it's on the mornings I want to give up, when God performs the biggest miracles.

One Wednesday morning the mother of one of our students called me. Her son had been struggling with thoughts of suicide. She called to let me know he would be coming to youth group tonight. As the mom's voice continued, my internal monologue started: *Oh no! I can't do it. I hate the feeling of responsibility that comes with suicidal ideation. God no!* And then the monologue was interrupted by the mom's earnest compliment: *There is no other place he would rather be tonight. Is that OK?* And what else could I say but *yes,* because that is the house I always wanted to own. The house where everyone is welcome, and we are always glad you came.

The widow had such an open home that in the middle of a drought she invited Elijah to stay with her. Elijah was a safe person, joining with the marginalized, the broken, and the disconnected. Elijah was a safe person, bringing God's word to the widow, and Elijah's words were honored by God. He was present in the state of drought, signaling God's heavenly provision. In the ancient world, the eyes of the community on the widow would have felt unrelenting. Often the eyes of our neighbors can feel overwhelming today. Elijah follows the pattern that Jesus exemplifies in the *New Testament.* Jesus bent down to look the innocent, infirm, and insignificant in the eye.

How do we do this thing called boundaries? How do we open up and risk like Elijah, the widow, and Jesus? How do we step back into relationship when we have been hurt? Let's stop and reflect on the current state of our relationships and look to God to figure out the how.

This circles graphic is a tool to help identify healthy relationships. It is an example of how the circles activity works.

This graphic is a tool for identifying healthy relationships. The picture below is an example of some common relationships we may have. It gives us a way to reflect on the question: Who is a safe person?

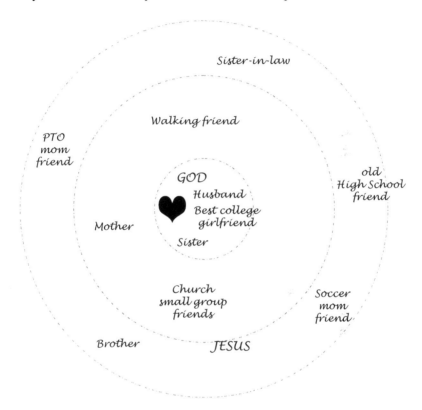

I have literally done this activity 50 times. Believe it or not, the people in my circles change. Every time I fill in the circles I discover something new about my relationships. Each time I reflect on the picture, I see an opportunity where I can grow. The biggest ahha moment I have had with Elijah's story and boundaries, is when the widow and Elijah met at the city gate. She chose to let him in. Elijah called from outside the gate and she chose to open it. This image empowered me. The widow didn't have to share water and bread. She didn't have to open the gate. Ultimately, the widow didn't have to obey God. I don't have to exercise boundaries. I don't have to seek God to guide my relationships. I don't have to be empowered by God. I can stay locked in a place of relational victimization.

For years I held a false theology that told me being a good Christian meant I was a doormat. I opened the door to my heart and let folks waltz in and rip and tear me to shreds. God didn't rip and tear me, the people in my life did! God instructs, *do not to throw pearls before swine.* In other words don't share your precious stories with untrustworthy people. God instructs *do not be like a dog who returns to his vomit.* In other words, don't keep going back to the same sick relationship and expect it to magically change and be healthy. God kept the widow in safety behind the fortification of the city wall. God has invited us to be safe under His wing, behind His gate, following His directions.

Be content with what you have, because God has said, "Never will I leave you; never will I forsake you." So we say with confidence, "The Lord is my helper; I will not be afraid."
– *Hebrews 13:5-6 NIV*

These circles are a tool to help you identify healthy and unhealthy relationships. Use the graphic to conduct a relationship inventory. Fill in the circles from the outside, in. The third ring is for people who know you, but don't really know you (like as a CEO or as someone's spouse). The second ring is for people who know you, but don't really know you (like as a soccer mom or a committee member in the community). The center circle is for people who know you (they know your heart). Don't overthink this activity. Just fill in the circles as names come to mind.

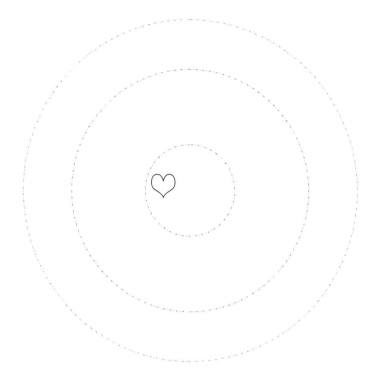

    I have had times when I stared at the blank circles and couldn't think of a single person's name to put inside. As a social worker, I have been educated to understand the importance of relationship connections. As a Christian I understand that God created us for community. And scientists tell us that friends are the catalyst for high points in any given day. The presence of a friend can make some of the most tedious activities enjoyable. Strong social relationships are the leading indicator of overall happiness. Sometimes it feels counterintuitive to invite connection when it can cause unimaginable heartache.

    Depending upon where you find yourself in the life circle of a friendship, one circle may be more full than another. The third circle may be full while the center circle is sparse, or vice versa. Take a few moments to reflect on your relationship circles. The final step is to go back and take a look at the names you have written.

    Honestly evaluate your relationships. Ask yourself this question: The last time I saw this person when I left them *I felt filled up or drained*. Are the people in your inner circle healthy relationships? Are the friendships mutual? How many people do you have in your inner circle? Author and speaker Brené Brown challenges her readers that the names of our closest friends should fit on a 2"x2" piece of paper. Use a pencil to draw a line pointing any unsafe people in your inner circle away from your heart. Now look at the names written in your other circles. Are any of those people life giving? Do they embody Dr. Cloud and Dr. Townsend's characteristics of a safe person? If so, draw an arrow pointing them toward the center circle. Put the date somewhere near the circle so that you can reflect on your circles again in the future.

I often do this activity when I am teaching the lesson on safe and unsafe people. It is an excellent evaluation tool. One time when I was teaching about safe people, after I filled in my circles they seemed very empty. I stared and stared wondering who was missing. I finally flipped back in my binder to look at a picture I had made in the past and discovered I had left off my entire family of origin. Looking at it all in black and white, I realized that I had some unresolved conflict between myself and someone in my family. I wasn't feeling safe and my subconscious did the work of keeping them off my circles. Reflecting on these relationships show me an area that I needed to reconcile. It wasn't an easy step, but it was definitely worthwhile because my family is very important to me.

God is added to the middle circle because when I first started teaching this activity He often was left off the circles. I believe it is important to include Him because He takes up space. God commands us to put nothing and no one before Him. He asks us to put Him first. God is also in the center circle because He is the only truly safe being that exists in this world. He is both the best example of a friend and the only One who has the capacity to never leave us or forsake us.

Jesus is the one true best friend. Whether we find ourselves alone for three years in the Kerith Ravine like Elijah, or we find ourselves on Mount Carmel surrounded by fans, God is our one true best friend. Dr. Cloud and Dr. Townsend describe three characteristics of a safe person. First, a safe person draws us closer to God. Second, a safe person draws us closer to others. And finally, a safe person helps us become the real person God created us to be. In Christ we find three qualities of a safe person: dwelling, grace, and truth. Jesus is the truest example of a best friend.

God provided companionship for the widow through Elijah. He protected the widow through daily provision. He promised to care for us more than He cares for the lilies of the field and birds of the air. He has given us a way to live that while hard, leads to harmony. God loves us. He created our hearts to be fleshy, vulnerable, powerful muscles that fuel life. He is desperate for us to bring our pile of broken glass so He can reassemble it. He wants the big and small shards of red blown glass so that He can take His Almighty crazy glue and put the pieces back together. He is dwelling, grace, and peace that will energize and equip us to be like Him, *Safe People*. By following God's design, we can be safe people and we can find safe people to commune with.

Psychologists have found that it takes an average of five positives to counteract every one negative. It is important to remember that we all go through tough, stressful times. We shouldn't kick people out of our lives because they are struggling. In fact, we all will have difficult times where we need support. But we need something to give those who are struggling. Allow God to use your community to pour into you and nurture your soul. And then pour back.

Provision to Ponder

Now, try re-doing your circles with the following directions: Move from the center out, based on time spent with people, defining the closeness of your relationship on time spent together. For instance, if you work full-time you may spend the most time during the week with co-workers. If you are a stay-at-home mom, maybe you spend the most adult time with other moms. Now, put a plus or minus next to each name based on whether you left your time feeling filled up or drained.

Take a moment to think about the relationships in your life. Write the names of your friends from your closest relationship to your more superficial. The first circle is for those you truly trust. The second circle is for people you know, but who don't know all your secrets. And the final circle is for people who know you, but don't really know you. That circle is for the soccer and PTO moms, the people on your dart league. Don't overthink it, just write and let all the names pour out.

Grab a pencil with an eraser and use the sample graphic as a guide to fill in your own circles.

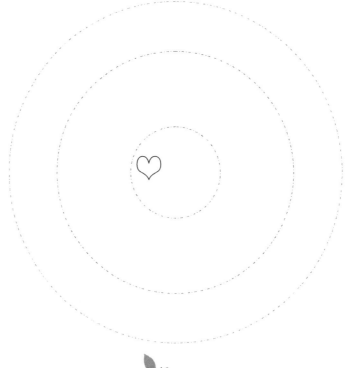

Allow God to nurture you by being mindful to spend time with a positive person this week. Take a step by scheduling time for coffee or lunch, invite one of the people who has a positive sign next to their name. This exercise is a good relationship maintenance tool.

🕊 List the characteristics of a good friend.

🕊 List some good friends.

🕊 Are you a good friend? How could you take a step to be a better friend?

Chapter 5

What Have I Done Wrong?

I grew up a pastor's kid. It was not part of my plan to become a pastor's wife. In fact, I married an optician turned business coach. It wasn't until one year after we got married that he came home from work one day and said: *I think I am called to go to seminary.*

I have now spent the better part of 15 years as a reluctant pastor's wife. I vowed I would do it differently. I never intended to let the congregation put me in a glass box. I never intended to allow myself to feel subjugated or judged by our parishioners. Yet, I ended up experiencing all of those feelings and more. Against *Pastor Wife* advice, I chose church members as friends. I attempted to integrate my life where my friends and our vocation were fully connected. At some point in that process, my dreams and reality collided and I found myself in a world of pain. I couldn't quite figure out who was a fan and who was a critic. Sometimes, I received both criticism and encouragement from the same person in the same sentence.

I got to the point where I hated to go to church. I sat stage left a few rows from the front. I appreciated my seat because generally only the musicians sat in front of me and I didn't have to watch people around me. In fact I re,ally couldn't see anyone from my seat. I felt like the X-ray vision of my critics bore a deep hole into the back of my head. I tried to find every way to help in children's ministry or do childcare rather than attend service. And worst of all, I couldn't figure out how to talk about it. I felt like I couldn't trust anyone. God had not told us to leave the church. He continued to affirm that we were to stay. But as each Sunday passed, it felt more and more unbearable. I wondered if safe people even existed. For a year I lived feeling disconnected, and experienced a drought in my friendships.

> **"What do you have against me, man of God? Did you come to remind me of my sin and kill my son?"**
> **– *1 Kings 17:18 NIV***

Elijah, the widow, and her son all enjoyed God's provision of fresh bread for some time, until one day they didn't. The Bible says that the widow's son became ill, and he grew so ill that his breath left him. He died. Every day, the widow had watched God provide flour and oil. But on this day, it wasn't provision she watched. Instead it was a deep withdrawal, the death of her only son. The widow did not mask her grief. She did not edit her thoughts. She lashed out at Elijah saying: *Oh man of God did you come here to remind me of all my sin and take away my son?* She accused God of punishing her for her past sins.

The widow had a moment of holy vulnerability. Her precious son was gone. Her last sinew of connection to society was gone. Her trust was gone. She had shared, she had risked, she had invited Elijah in and now he had betrayed her by allowing her son to die. The woman highlighted in Elijah's story is described by her social status. As a widow, this woman has absolutely no value to her community. Her only value is as the mother of her child. The loss of her son threatened to hurl her into a desolate place of disconnection and loneliness.

The very word *widow* means a person who is shamed. The definition of connection is feeling valued, accepted, worthy, and affirmed; while disconnection is the feeling of being diminished, rejected, unworthy, and reduced. (Dan Allender, *To Be Told*, 77) Elijah communing with the woman moved her from a place of disconnection, rejection, and unworthiness to a place of worthiness, value, and connection. God sent Elijah to a widow. This is not an accident or happenstance. He prepared the widow and sent Elijah. God protected the widow by providing connection which was countercultural in that day. God directed Elijah to an isolated, shamed, social reject in keeping with God's model of service to the least of these.

I was that widow. If God is the God of connection, why did I feel so alone? It felt so miserable, as though there was a microscope over me, zooming in to reveal all my faults. I felt isolated. My ordinary life felt mundane and boring. The routine I had thrived on was leaving me empty and unstimulated. WHY?

"What have I done wrong," asked Obadiah, "that you are handing your servant over to Ahab to be put to death?"
– 1 Kings 18:9 NIV

So, the next part of the story is another invasion of darkness and another opportunity to ask *Why?* Obadiah is the King's right-hand man. Obadiah who has chutzpah all his own, gets up off his knees and squares off with Elijah. He questions how after all he has done, this could happen. In the face of meeting God's legendary prophet, Obadiah's emotions quickly change from honor to fear. *He is thrown into a similar conflict as the widow.* He instantly questions what he has done wrong instead of what God might put right through the meeting and Elijah's requests. This story highlights our fallen nature.

I resonate with Obadiah. I am on my knees professing my faith to God and I am distracted by the buzz of my phone. The texts, Facebook posts, Twitter comments take me off track and suddenly I am comparing and contrasting my life with someone else's. I find myself saying: *God don't you remember all I have done for you? I led that Bible study. I opened my home for prayer meeting. I took care of the kids while my husband traveled, ate out, and stayed in hotels. I HAVE SERVED YOU! What have I done wrong that you would ask me to stay on my knees, face down, and worship? Why won't you give me what's mine? Why won't you reward me?*

Just as God turned the widow's world upside down, He did the same for Obadiah. The question: *What have I done wrong?* is rooted in a deeper question: *Why isn't it going the way I thought it would?* This is the only weapon Satan has. He is not God, although he was close to God. Our enemy is present today and knows the past, but he does not know our future. As a fallen angel, Lucifer's cohorts (the angels) are tight with God to this day, but he is not. He is the ruler of this world, not the world to come. So, as the ruler of this world, his job is to convince us that we are the rulers of our own destiny too. He is cajoling, trying to convince us that today is the only day we have. And when things don't turn out as we hope for or imagine, he exploits the angst in our heart and turns it to doubt in God.

Remember the garden. Adam and Eve were instructed by God not to eat from the tree of good and evil because it would kill them. The snake slithered into Eve's mind and said: *Is that really what God said? Are you sure you will die?* He used question and doubt to cause Eve to stumble. Satan is no less crafty today.

There is a compelling portrayal of Satan's use of shame and doubt in Mel Gibson's, *The Passion of the Christ*. During the brutal scourging scene when Jesus is tied to a post and being whipped mercilessly by the Roman guards, we see a powerful juxtaposition. We see Mary, Jesus' widowed earthly mother, watching, crying, helpless to protect her child. Mary is standing in a mob of people which includes John the brother of Jesus and Mary Magdalene. She vacillates between horror and devastation as she watches for a moment and then holds her face in her hands. Tears drench the dirt beneath her feet. Through the crowd we watch Satan slither. The dark hooded character is beautifully horrific. He glides through the people caressing a shriveled distressed-looking man-baby in his arms. Mary and Satan lock eyes gazing across the most intense, sacrificial act of all time. Satan says without using words: *Don't you love your son? Do something. I am carrying my child and look, he is safe. Aren't you going to come for your child? Where is your God now?* Satan gazes straight through Jesus begging the question: *Where is your protector and provider now?* For those moments does Mary feel abandoned by God? Jesus, the vulnerable image of God, in flesh appears to be abandoned by His Heavenly Father.

Satan is so cunning. He moves through our lives planting questions and placing slivers of doubt. He swaddles his own and demonstrates his limited power by allowing the wicked to prosper. And he asks the question: *Why isn't your God protecting and providing for you now?*

Shame is a powerful weapon. In the Garden of Eden shame did two powerful things. Shame separated Adam and Eve from each other. Once walking with each other in the garden face-to-face, they end up back-to-back, accused and covered up. Not only are they separated from each other, shame also separated Adam and Eve from God. When God came for His daily walk with them in the cool of the day, they were covered up and hiding. God called to them and asked what they had done. Adam wags his finger at God and then Eve: *The woman you gave me gave me the fruit.*

Shame is a powerful weapon very present today. Shame can mask many different emotions, most commonly fear. It makes sense that Satan's haunting circular question would be: *How did your past choice make this bad thing happen?* But God doesn't work that way. He has searched us and knows our inner-most thoughts. He already knows what we think before we think it. His desire is for us to confess our thoughts to Him so He can make us whole. Shame prefers darkness. I have found that one way to unlock the power of shame is to imagine it like a mask. Imagine if you were wearing a mask so everyone could see what you felt like when you felt ashamed. My shame thoughts are: *You're not as good as that other person. There is someone prettier, smarter, more organized, and skinnier than you who will do a better job than you.* Inside I feel torn, exposed, embarrassed. I feel like everyone can see what I look like under my clothes. The pictures below provide a visual to the illusive experience of shame. The left circle depicts how shame affects me on the inside. The right circle depicts how I present shame to the outside world. It is interesting how different the same emotion can be.

I have deep stretch marks on my upper hips. I also have long stretch marks across my lower abdomen. Some came from a growth spurt in high school but most were exquisitely chiseled with each of my three pregnancies. My third daughter earned the nickname pinch because she would rub her finger along my stretch marks and pinch me while she was nursing. She found it self-soothing. I found it incredibly vulnerable. Rubbing those marks brought her comfort while exposing one of my weaknesses. I don't look like a super model. I have cellulite in places where it doesn't belong. Having my daughter exploit my weakness didn't feel good. It pressed me to acknowledge my imperfection. When she would rub my stretch marks I couldn't pretend they were not there.

Sometimes I would ask her to stop. She would look up at me with the biggest brown eyes and say: *But I like it.* And that says it all. The masks I wear before God and others are a cover for the beauty of my vulnerability. God sees the whole package. He knows where I struggle. And He likes me. He desires to be glorified through my struggle. That can't happen if I cover up and hide. God is light. Darkness scatters in the face of light. Shame scatters in the face of truth. Shame is the ultimate separator. God is the Supreme Uniter.

"Is that you, you troubler of Israel?"
– *1 Kings 18:17 NIV*

I wonder if the widow's breath left her too, when her boy died. Elijah didn't say a word. He gathered her precious connector in his arms and ran up the stairs to lay him before God. The widow followed him. After her shaming outburst, she flew into action waiting expectantly to see what this Man of God would do. Elijah prayed and the boy's breath came back. The widow in a moment of transparent disbelief says: *God you are my God.*

Elijah reassured Obadiah of God's protection. He swore the protection of God's angels on him. And Obadiah obeyed. Obadiah told King Ahab that the drought was going to end. Obadiah announced Elijah's arrival and lived.

This is a pivotal place in the story. Elijah has obeyed. He has walked through the three-year drought, encouraging others as he went. And now, he is directed back to his nemesis King Ahab to fulfill God's plan. Elijah approaches the king, and from a distance Ahab calls: *Is that you, you troubler of Israel?* Unlike the reactions of the widow and Obadiah, there is no wavering, no wash of shame for Elijah. He confidently responds: *I have not made trouble for Israel, but you and your father's family have. You have abandoned the Lord's commands and have followed the Baals.*

Elijah's clear, concise response is inspiring. Unfortunately for me, my shame reaction often leaves me frozen with no coherent thoughts to share. Maybe you are like me. Our culture clamors for our attention. Our work keeps us busy. And in that busyness we can lose sight of who we are listening to. The art of reflection allows us to recognize where we are stuck, shift our relationships to meet the current needs we have, and untangle the messages Satan has been feeding us. Below is a place for you to reflect. Use the blank shame masks on the next page to help you process how shame affects you.

Provision to Ponder

The Shame Mask

Left: Identify what shame feels like inside of you. Imagine if you were wearing a mask so everyone could see what you feel like when you feel ashamed. What is your shame message? Using the widow and Obadiah as examples, identify how shame thoughts are triggered in you.

Right: Identify what you look like to others when you feel shame. Identify what you let others see when you feel ashamed.

Where is Satan lurking in your thoughts and keeping you in bondage?

Today, what parts of your body, soul, and spirit feel dark?

Identify a step you can take to invite light.

Spend a few moments in prayer. As you pray unclench your hands, release control to God. Hold your hands upright, with your palms facing the ceiling. Ask God to reveal where Satan is shaming you and keeping you in bondage to his lies.

Identify what you are holding too tightly.

Identify where you need to invite God to be your *Protector and Provider.*

Chapter 6

The Idol Limp

Elijah went before the people and said,
"How long will you waver between two opinions?
If the Lord is God, follow him;
but if Baal is god, follow him."
– *1 Kings 18:21 NIV*

Even as a little girl I was vividly aware of the people around me.
Growing up as pastor's kids, my siblings and I were mindful that people
were always watching. From as young as I can remember I despised
coffee hour, that time when I had to figure out how to do small talk.
I felt obligated to accept hugs from people. It seemed like the right
thing to do. I was an introverted kid who struggled with the politics
of pastoring. When I was young I didn't have a name for the things I
struggled with. It wasn't until sometime in my 30s that the feeling was
validated and given a name: *people pleasing*.

I not only learned how to people please, I discovered that I was very
good at it. I was an overachiever at people pleasing. I figured out how
to muster up the courage to shake hands long enough that people felt
cared for. I practiced certain sound bites to help extend conversations.
I learned how to get the attention off of me and onto the other person. I
attentively listened while folks disarmed and divulged. Looking back, I
think this was training ground for my future counseling days. As coffee
hours turned into cocktail parties, I learned how to muster enough
bravery to walk through the front door, scan the room for a safe face,
and get myself into a conversation.

My cocktail hour tactics and people pleasing excellence worked for
35 years. I give credit for a decade of the success, between 25 and 35,
to being married to the best wooer in the business. My husband became
a beautiful buffer. He was empathetic, kind, and charismatic. He had

no problem opening the door and leading me into the party by the arm. I could stand quietly, smiling while he navigated the room. I believe my breakdown would have come much sooner if I hadn't been married to him. But one day the years of stuffing my emotions exploded and I found myself gripped with panic. One day it all came crashing down. I describe my panic feeling as if someone wearing boots was standing on my chest. My head tells me I am OK but my body acts like I am having a heart attack. My body gasps for breath even though I can breathe.

I had my first panic attack far from home. I was 37 years old, on vacation with our family. We were enjoying the Colorado Springs area. My husband had planned to run part of Pike's Peak, but his health didn't cooperate so we compromised and drove the mountain pass instead. The air was clear, the sun was bright, the road was open, and we were on an adventure. We began our ascent. We had just visited the *Focus on the Family* bookstore and purchased the dramatized CD set for *The Chronicles of Narnia*. Our three kids were completely engaged in the story. My husband and I chatted, listened, and looked. I remember noticing a small road sign that read: *End of tree line*. The posting meant nothing to me, until it did.

We continued to drive up the mountain watching as the dense forest made way to bare ground with few trees. The further we traveled, the narrower the road became. As if it had happened in an instant, my passenger window revealed an overlook that went down for miles. My fear of heights activated and I became agitated. In 30 seconds my tone went from calm to anxious. I begged my husband to pull over. He responded quietly at first, gently explaining that there was nowhere for him to go. The cars were backed up single file while we slowly approached the peak. There was no shoulder on the road. I squirmed, looked away, and finally lay prostrate between the two front seats of our van. My husband now agitated, forcefully directed me to be quiet because my panic was making him so nervous he was struggling to drive.

Meanwhile, our two-year-old daughter sat in her car seat almost leaning out of the car to look over the edge. As she enjoyed the view she stroked my head saying: *Mommy it's OK. It's beautiful. Look, it's beautiful.* I lay face down using every meditation skill I had ever learned. I prayed. I called on God's name. I panted, breathed, and panted. Once at the top, I walked laps around the gift shop and prayed that I would make it down alive.

I've shared this story a lot. Someone somewhere heard my story and named it. *You had a panic attack*, they said. Unfortunately that experience triggered a few years of intermittent panic attacks, never as severe as the *Pike's Peak Panic*, but noticeable enough that I had to do something. The *Pike's Peak Panic* was triggered by my fear of heights. The rest of my panic experiences were triggered by people; mostly encounters with people where I had to disagree with them, or lead in a different direction than they wanted, or during conflict when someone was expressing displeasure in me or questioning my judgment. After the *Pike's Peak Panic*, I was triggered by *People Pleasing Panic*. And it was so bad it almost defeated me.

People had become my idols. An idol is a false messenger bringing comfort, direction, or leading devoid of God. An idol is anything that we put more value in than God. An idol is something that we worship. In the *New Testament* the apostle Paul writes: *we know that "an idol has no real existence," and that "there is no God but one." For although there may be so-called gods n heaven or on earth—as indeed there are many "gods" and many "lords"—yet for us there is one God ... and one Lord, Jesus Christ.*

Paul is speaking to the Corinthians who are just learning about Jesus. Traditional worship in the ancient world included a pantheon of gods. When Abraham left the gods of his father he was leaving polytheistic worship—the worship of many gods. The Jewish God of Abraham, Isaac, and Jacob was monotheistic. This was revolutionary. Christianity follows that tradition. Paul is speaking to Jew and Gentile converts to Christ. These are people who have grown up in a culture that worships a pantheon of gods.

I believe the greatest danger that cultural Christians struggle with today is that we don't think we need to worry about idols. It is easy to dismiss the idea of modern day idol worship. It feels like an antiquated idea. By definition, the act of idolizing is to put something first. It is the act of putting something in front of God, to value something more than you value God. In ancient times people made gods for the harvest, wind, sun, or love, which is not far from our modern day gods of control, relationships, and possessions.

Every morning when I wake up I have a choice. I can choose to follow me and make decisions that will fulfill my personal desires and the desires of my family. Or, I can wake up, climb out of bed, and follow Jesus. Living for Jesus is counter-cultural. Christ bent down and washed his disciples' feet. He touched the untouchable and spoke words of hope to the hopeless, like the widows. He valued the outcasts. It is easy to skip over the passage on idolatry as irrelevant, when in fact there has never been a time in United States history where we have embraced more idols. We have a television show called: *American Idol*. We idolize Hollywood stars, cars (for me the Honda Odyssey), a dream home, a dream spouse, and ideal children. We idolize a job, a look, an image, and quickly become more and more captivated by that picture, until it becomes what we meditate on day and night.

A while ago I went to a meeting for a multi-level marketing company. The coach was encouraging us to identify what we really wanted—the car, the house, or the ideal weight—and cut out magazine pictures of those things to hang all over the house. These images were to inspire us toward our goals. For a moment I was caught up in the idea. In fact, I found an old picture of myself. It was a picture of my husband and me in front of Elvis' Graceland Mansion. I was a pre-baby svelte size six. I made that picture my goal. I wanted to look like that again. The picture stayed on my refrigerator for a long time. That picture symbolized an image from part of my life years before. After years of frustrating yo-yo dieting and little success, I replaced that picture with a prayer for my husband:

> Lord, thank you for my husband,
> I ask Your will for him in these things,
> according to Your Word.

The prayer card included verses designed to compel him, empower him, equip him, supply for him, and guide him. Shifting the focus from my outward appearance to the condition of my heart changed the way I carried myself and the way I saw myself. It made me more desirable than if I was suddenly a smaller size. It changed how I viewed myself as a wife and as a woman. It changed how I treated my husband.

"Is that you, you troubler of Israel?"
– 1 Kings 18:17 NIV

After a long time, in the third year, God came to Elijah again and commanded him to tell Ahab that the drought was about to end. When Ahab saw Elijah he called him a *troublemaker for Israel*. King Ahab blamed Elijah for the trouble that had come upon the Israelites. Elijah delivered on his promise to Obadiah and was obedient to God when he delivered his last message to the king. Elijah confidently responded by holding Ahab accountable. He called out Ahab and his family as the true troublemakers for abandoning God's commands and following Baal. Elijah instructed Ahab. Pause for a moment and take in the scene. The king of Samaria who blames Elijah for the folly of his country now stands at attention as Elijah gives him a directive: *Now summon the people from all over Israel to meet me on Mount Carmel. And bring the four hundred and fifty prophets of Asherah, who eat at Jezebel's table.*

The prophets of Baal were invited to a showdown on Mount Carmel.

Elijah came near to all the people and said, "How long will you halt *and* limp between two opinions? If the Lord is God, follow Him; but if Baal, follow him." And the people did not answer him a word.
– 1 Kings 18:21 AMP

Jezebel's prophets gathered on Mount Carmel, then built an altar, tormented themselves, called out to their gods, and prayed for fire. Baal was a Canaanite god of rain, thunder, lightening, and dew. It is significant that while experiencing the drought Jezebel's kingdom was worshiping Baal. Up on Mount Carmel the prophets of Baal prayed for fire, but nothing happened. All day the people watched the prophets of Baal cut themselves attempting to get Baal's attention.

The Hebrew word for *limping* or *waver* is the same as the word used for *danced*.

Then they called on the name of Baal from morning till noon. "Baal, answer us!" they shouted. But there was no response; no one answered. And they danced around the altar they had made.
– 1 Kings 18:26 NIV

The verse depicts the prophets of Baal frantically dancing around their altar. Elijah spoke with sharp irony. In the religious ambivalence of Israel, the Israelites also engaged in a wild and futile religious *dance*. In this story, it seems absurd that the prophets would dance around frantically calling out to a false god. It feels absurd until we realize we are doing it ourselves. I have danced around a false god rationalizing how a bigger, better, more expensive house—one that we could not afford—would make me feel whole and more alive. I have danced for bigger bedrooms that would give my children a better life. I have danced about how driving a Honda Odyssey would keep me safe and save me money. Why, I would feel complete in a better car, even if the car cost more than we could afford. Dancing around the altar of this world takes our eyes off ushering in Christ's Kingdom.

And Jesus says:

"Very truly I tell you, no servant is greater than his master, nor is a messenger greater than the one who sent him. "
– John 13:16 NIV

His reign is counter-cultural: the last will be first and the servant is made greater than his master.

"So the last will be first, and the first will be last."
– Matthew 20:16 NIV

What altar am I dancing around today?

And they took the bull that was given them, and they prepared it and called upon the name of Baal from morning until noon, saying, "O Baal, answer us!" But there was no voice, and no one answered.
– 1 Kings 18:26 ESV

As the prophets of Baal continued to bargain with their false gods, they yelled louder and they stumbled around the altar they had made. They cut themselves. I had heard this story throughout my childhood. I often wondered why the prophets cut themselves. As a kid I thought it was weird that anyone would purposefully hurt themselves, especially in worship. I guess it was a similar mental conundrum for which I suspended my disbelief: *Why was Abraham willing to sacrifice his son?* What god would require such behavior?

It became real when I learned that in the United States teenagers were cutting. Teens and young adults use razor blades, not to kill themselves, but instead to relieve their pain by feeling the pain of their own skin slicing apart. I have worked with teens that cut their arms and legs, and they describe the experience as a huge relief. The cutting collides with their otherwise numb existence and allows them to feel even if just for a moment. I wonder if the prophets of Baal were doing the same thing. They worshipped a false god. They cried out to him. They were giving their lives to him, yet they didn't feel anything. Their god was distant and disconnected from their daily lives. Their god was not real. For Christ followers it is difficult to understand this. Our God is present. He is active and through His Spirit we truly feel Him. His Spirit moves in us. The juxtaposition of the two gods is startling. Again the God of Abraham, Isaac, and Jacob is alive and does things very differently.

Re-entering the story we find Elijah making fun of the false prophets. He suggested that Baal was relieving himself or on vacation. All the while Baal's prophets mutilated themselves waiting for the god of rain, thunder, lightening, and dew to answer. Later that day Elijah asked for help rebuilding his altar. He took twelve stones to represent the twelve tribes of Israel. Elijah had a trench dug around his altar. He had the offering, the wood, and the trench drenched with water. The Scripture says the trench was filled to overflowing.

Remember the land continues to experience drought. This is remarkable. Elijah asked for a rare commodity, water to be virtually wasted. Instead of drinking the water, they drenched the wood and the offering. The onlookers watch as water flowed over the altar and filled the trench around it. Remember that the people watching were in need of water for themselves. It is the middle of a drought. This is a remarkable move of audacity or faith—or maybe audacious faith. God promised to end the drought. Elijah acts in faith of God's provision when he has his servants spend water valued like gold and waste it. I originally thought Elijah was a bad steward. But I have discovered that below Mount Carmel is the Dead Sea, so the water they are using is salt water, not suitable for drinking. And Elijah then prayed.

"O Lord, God of Abraham, Isaac, and Jacob, let it be known today that You are God in Israel and that I am your servant ..."
– *1 Kings 18:36 NIV*

Elijah called down fire from heaven. The wet offering was engulfed with flames. Just like when he healed the widow's son, Elijah was the conduit, the servant, the vessel, the faithful one. God did the miracle through his faithful obedient servant, Elijah.

> **When all the people saw this, they fell prostrate and cried, "The Lord—he is God. The Lord—he is God" … And Elijah said to Ahab, "Go, eat and drink, for there is the sound of a heavy rain."**
> **– *1 Kings 18:39, 41 NIV***

The people echoed the words of the widow: *The Lord—he is God*. It is significant that the people recognize and glorify God in the miracle. God will not share His glory. He desires that we honor Him as our *Protector* and *Provider* at all times.

While the Baal worshippers danced and the people limped wavering between two gods, the God of Abraham, Isaac, and Jacob acted. He sent fire from heaven and incinerated the offering in a dazzling miraculous display of His power. God the *Protector* and *Provider* protected Elijah from the prophets of Baal, from the crowd, and from an angry king. He provided stamina and clear thinking for Elijah. He also provided fire from heaven to prove His existence.

Provision to Ponder

Take a highlighter, pen, or pencil, and identify which names of God resonate with you. Then go back through your list and star your top three names of God.

Fruit Bearer   Gracious Giver   Wellspring   Tabernacle

Hope   Most High   Alpha   Power   Name Above Names

Sanctification   Builder   Almighty   Authority

Prince of Life   The Way

Master   Life   Indwelling   New Song

Maker   Overcomer   Great Gift   Kind King

Servant   Creator   Revelation   Christ

Savior   The Coming One   Majesty

Love   Kinsman   Shiloh   Awesome God

Salvation

Dwelling Place   Inheritance   Silent Shield   Jesus   Belt of Truth

Provider   Infinite   Christ our Savior

Always There   Our Victory   Wisdom   Elohim

Vanquisher   Incarnate   Intercessor

Quickener   Worthy   Bread of Life   Eternal

Jewel

Praise Worthy   Carpenter   Israel's Joy   Beautiful Crown

Magnificent   Omnipotent   Just Judge

Encourager   Boundless   Debt Payer   Guardian

The King of Kings

Good Shepherd   Jehovah   Strong Standard

Omniscient

Altogether Lovely   Sanctuary   Repairer   Shalom

Counselor   Beloved Son   Good Guide

Redemption

Advocate   Hope of Glory   Supplier   Sufficient

Perfector   Omega   Rescuer   Atonement

Example El Shaddai Leader Pierced

Only Begotten Refuge Receiver Ransom All in All

Unchangeable Physician Immanuel

Consolation Discipler Friend of sinners

Sufferer Water of Lie Governor King of the Jews

Forerunner Salt

Spring of Joy Unmovable Minister Messiah

Reprover Goodness Chosen Refiner

Exalted Yesterday Comforter Helmet Healer

Lawgiver Today Tomorrow

Potter Barrier Breaker Redeemer

Foundation Conquerer Resurrection Crucified

I Am Refresher

Root

Undefeated Destroyer

Eagle's Wing Pearl Prince of Peace Queller of Storms

Fisher of Men

Rock Cornerstone All Reigning

Hope of Hopes

Bountiful Passover Lamb Yahweh Appointed Heir

Olive Tree

Head of the Church Supplier Compassionate Star of Jacob

God of Cherubim Divine Ruler

Omnipresent

Son of Man Precious Restorer Triumphant

Rose of Sharon Reformer Holy One Merciful

Warrior Father

Offering Protector Bright and Truth Yoke Fellow

Wonderful Teacher

Burden Bearer Morning Star Word of God

Right Hand

Righteousness Amazing Grace Fulfiller Fountain

Soul Defender

Glorified Jesse's Root Solid Rock

Living One

Hiding Place Sovereign Bridegroom

Abba

Write your top three names of God on a sticky note. Place the list on your bathroom mirror or on the dashboard of your car. Use this is as a re-centering tool when you are tempted to slip back into habits of control, worry, or panic.

Take a moment to reflect on how God has protected and provided for you.

🕊 What do you put your faith in?

🕊 Where are you limping and leaning on a crutch (idol)? How are you trying to take care of yourself?

🕊 Take a moment to reflect on how God has protected and provided for you this week. List even the little things: the sun, a home, a warm meal, a friend.

Chapter 7

The Many Faces of Fear

My seven-year-old self walked from patchwork to patchwork within my quilt. It was as if the colors came alive. The paisley swirl enveloped me. The flowers invited me to frolic. But the dream always ended as a nightmare. The angry jaws of a lion salivated as he closed his mouth over my foot. The jarring experience would shake me awake, to find myself tangled in my once welcoming quilt, somewhere near the bottom of my bed. There I would shake, closing and opening my eyes to remind myself it was only a dream. My feet would feel like pins and needles, they had fallen asleep. Closing my eyes tight, I would shake and wiggle trying to make the lion go away.

As a little girl that is what fear looked like to me. Fear lurked in the darkness. It lingered in the silence. I learned how to navigate my fear—living with the pit in my stomach—though never was my fear truly gone.

Elijah was so strong. Throughout the story he had stared down fear and watched God deliver. The first years of the drought experience Elijah spent in the desert. He was alone. He was provided for daily, but there was no warm hearth to hover over. I wonder if Elijah encountered hostile wild animals. We experience the illusion that the ravens were civilized servants to Elijah, like a flight attendant offering soda and a bag of pretzels to an airline customer. I wonder did the ravens toss meat and bread his way only to fight with him over dinner?

During college I went on a 10-day outward bound type experience called *Lavida*. Part of the challenge was to spend 48 hours alone in the woods with God, a lean-to, and toilet paper. Our guides warned us that often the smoothest places, the ones that look the most welcoming to make camp are actually deer beds. My first and only overnight in the wild included an unpleasant middle-of-the-night encounter. I woke up from a half-way sleep to find a deer staring me down. I had few options so I chose to just lie very still until the deer left. And it did. I slept the rest of the night with one eye open. Desert creatures include wild animals like jackals, foxes, lizards, and bats. How did Elijah sleep during those early years? As the drought continued and the animals were hungry, was Elijah a tasty diversion from starvation?

We don't hear in the biblical account the word fear—until Elijah meets Ahab on the road. His fellow sojourners, the widow and Obadiah both gasped as they panicked, each for their own reasons. During this time Elijah is not described with terms like worry, concern, or fear. But now, after God has sent fire from heaven, after the promise of provision, and after the hope of a happy ending—Elijah is afraid. He warns King Ahab to button down the hatches because the rain is coming and King Ahab brings those ominous words from his devilish queen: *If you are not dead by tonight, surely I will die.*

It is the threat of King Ahab's unstable counterpart, Queen Jezebel that sends Elijah running in fear. It appears that Elijah is terrified. There are so many words to describe fear, each taking on a different inflection. Under his circumstances Elijah runs away in fear. In my early years, I curled up, with the covers up to my chin, shaking the tingles out of my feet. As a 30-something when fear gripped me, I went straight to my phone. I used gossip as a way to increase my self-worth and push away the unpleasant, out-of-control feeling of fear.

Elijah and his servant ran. They ran a day's journey into the wilderness. Then the Bible notes that Elijah left his servant and ran another day's journey on his own. He mumbles words of anger and frustration to himself as he pants and staggers. He finds himself where he began. Alone in the desert, desperate to understand what his God was doing and how fulfillment of God's promise would come.

Often I find myself in situations where I wonder how I ended up in the place I find myself. I actually attempted to do things differently so that my outcome would be altered. One of the most valuable lessons I have learned is to share my feelings, in words, with a safe person. As soon as I feel emotion begin to bubble up in me, I try to articulate it with a feeling word. Unnamed the bubble often leads to a deep volcanic rumble that often erupts hurting me and those around me. It is the emotion that lies under the surface that gets tripped or triggered by an unsuspected situation and ends with toxic results.

Anger is a secondary emotion. Anger is the emotion that God gave us for protection. It is the emotion that indicates our will has been violated. Anger is the feeling of the rumble, the hot lava that lies below the surface. When it is activated our bodies respond physically. Imagine your child after you say *no*. Their will has been violated—probably for their safety and protection but they do not understand—and that boundary trips the trigger. When our children are two or three years old, they often respond by throwing a tantrum. Their will was violated so they get mad. As we grow older we develop more sophisticated ways of coping with unwelcome boundaries. We may learn to manipulate by giving the silent treatment or withdrawing our love or approval. When our will is thwarted, no matter our age, the feeling of injustice or wrong incites the BIG angry emotion.

If anger is the secondary emotion and is that powerful, what is the primary emotion? The primary emotion is generally fear. Every time an angel appeared to someone in the Bible the angel's first words were: *Do not be afraid.* Whenever God gave His people an important direction, He instructed them to not be afraid. When my sense of injustice is activated often the next emotion to overwhelm me is fear—the feeling of *I can't do this.* I think God comforts His people because our nature is to respond out of instinct. In clinical terms we have a *fight, flight, or freeze* response. In simple terms when we feel violated our brain shifts from ordered thought into survival mode. We are each unique creatures, so our *go to* responses are different. If our survival mode is to fight, we put up our dukes—either with fists or with words—and begin to fight. If our survival mode is flight, we run. This is manifested by physically leaving a conflictual situation. Finally, if your survival mode is to freeze—you might be physically present, but emotionally absent. I freeze when conflict erupts around me. You can see it on my shame mask in Chapter 5. I may be physically present outside, but inside my mind is a jumble. My heart beats rapidly and my palms sweat. I also struggle to maintain eye contact. My stomach churns and I have no words.

The next time you are with someone who becomes angry, look behind the rage. He or she probably feels out of control or insecure. People experiencing insecurity often struggle with anger. If this is you, there is hope. Security and insecurity take us back to Chapter 5. We are often the most insecure when we feel out of control. And when we feel out of control our natural coping method is to grab for one of our idols. As we have seen throughout Elijah's story, he looks to God. And that is the best solution for us as well. Grab for God!

This part of the story is no exception. Elijah is afraid. He runs. He grumbles and complains. He isolates. He ends up where he began. In the wilderness he lashes out at God. The Bible states that after his encounter with King Ahab, Elijah was afraid. But what are the first words we hear from Elijah? *Oh God let me go be with my ancestors.*

Elijah reacts with two instincts. He flees and while he is fleeing he begins to fight with God. He yells at God. His tone is intense. He is angry. Nothing has worked out the way he had imagined. And now he would rather go meet his ancestors—DIE—than journey on.

Let's take a moment and stop here. It is very uncomfortable to hang in this dissonance. Our prophet protagonist has surprised us. His story isn't turning out the way we might have imagined.

God has given us feeling words as a gift.

Words to describe our feelings are often illusive. Below are feeling dolls that provide a variety of words for each feeling category.

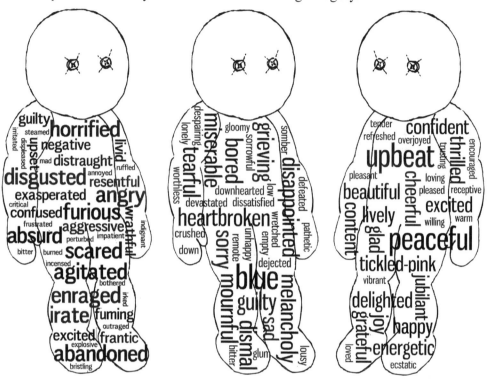

> Take a few moments to reflect on the feeling dolls.

> Identify three words in each category that are new or different from your typical *go to* words.

Provision to Ponder

Think back to your timeline in Chapter 1. Where is your story dark? Where is your story red with rage? Where is your story bitter? Take a few minutes to color the picture to reflect what fear looks like.

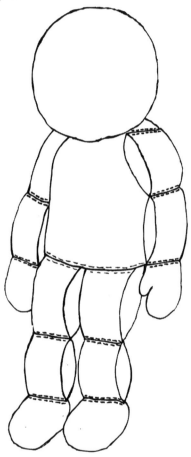

 What experiences evokes fear in you?

 What do you look like when you feel afraid?

 Describe a time when God protected and provided for you.

 Reflect: After this, the word of the Lord came to Abram in a vision: "Do not be afraid, Abram. I am your shield, your great reward." –*Genesis 15:1*

 What does it mean for God to be your shield?

Chapter 8

Finding a Broom Tree

And behold, an angel touched him …
— 1 Kings 19:5 ESV

I was lying in the bathtub. Crying. I felt nauseous. After finding no relief I went upstairs to go to bed. I crawled under the covers. Sobbing. My husband asked me what was wrong. My struggle didn't match my emotion. I had no words to explain what I was feeling. I felt overwhelmed. He was pensive. He asked me how I was feeling. I just feel sick! I guess on a normal night he might have tucked me into bed and let me cry myself to sleep. Crying is one of my most cathartic activities when words just don't do it. But this night was different. This night, I was 36 weeks pregnant and due for our third child.

He shuffled me off to the hospital. First, the doctor asked to give me an epidural.

No! I am doing this natural. I have a plan. It's all written down. There is supposed to be a birthing ball in the shower. You aren't the right doctor. Where is my doctor? The on-call doctor looked at me and said: *You will need to lie very still. You will not be taking a shower. We need to monitor the baby's heart.* No! This isn't the plan. Read MY plan!

Upon the information that I wouldn't be permitted to move for the most intense portion of labor, I quickly opted for the epidural. And then the room became a blur. The doctor said: *It's too late. There is no time.*

He looked at me, this strange doctor who I had never met, this man who didn't know the plan. He looked me in the eyes and said: *Do exactly what I say.*

My eyes big, I remember saying: *How can I? I can't feel anything.*

He looked intently at me and said: *Push.*

The swirl of activity continued as I pushed, breathed, tried to listen, and pushed again. The baby came out and the commotion ceased. Before I knew what happened the room was silent. No doctor, no nurse, no husband, no baby.

Everything is OK, came the gentle voice of a nurse, who began to clean me up. I physically felt great. The pain was gone. We chatted. She tended. And the fear in my heart grew. The reason I was there. The work of the past few hours. The reality that maybe, the baby wasn't OK. She smiled timidly from the end of the bed, trying to act confident. But I knew, she didn't know. Finally, the pediatrician came into the room. She said: *They are still cleaning up the baby. You can see her soon.*

Her, it was a her. And then the pediatrician said the words I was anxious to hear: *Your baby is perfect. Her Apgar scores are perfect. I've never been part of a birth that was so complicated when the baby was OK. She is your miracle.*

That pediatrician was my angel. She brought words of comfort. She brought words of peace. She brought words of hope. Elijah's angel met him in his loneliest, darkest, scariest moment and brought him comfort, peace, and hope.

**And behold, an angel touched him and said to him, "Arise and eat."
And he looked, and behold, there was at his head a cake baked on hot
stones and a jar of water. And he ate and drank and lay down again.
And the angel of the Lord came again a second time and touched him
and said, "Arise and eat, for the journey is too great for you."**
– *1 Kings 19:5-8 ESV*

Elijah had just asked God to let him die. He had just shaken an angry fist at his Maker. He had given up. And God sent him an angel under the broom tree.

Broom trees are very common in the Middle East. They are low to the ground and brushy. Their roots reach deep in the earth to tap into the water that is in short supply in the desert. The long spindly dry branches form a web, one that Elijah could rest under. The tree provided refuge. The roots of the broom tree would heat up during the day under the intense desert sun. The warm roots would release heat into the ground through the night, providing Elijah with warmth as the desert temperatures dropped after sunset. This is the place God provided for Elijah to find comfort, peace, and hope. God gave Elijah the gift of rest.

We were wired for rest from the very beginning. We were created in God's image. On the seventh day God rested. God didn't need to rest. He has infinite everything. But He chose to rest. And He modeled rest for us by instructing us to keep a Sabbath. There are a few dimensions of rest that are important to take into consideration. There is the rest of sleep, which scientists have found we need six to eight hours of daily. And there is the quality of rest which is relaxation and reinvigorating. In the creation story God rested by admiring all He had made. I believe He was celebrating His accomplishment. He was rejoicing in His good work. As people created in the image of God—given the powerful job of working to tend His world—we are responsible to take time to rest and admire our work. In our cultural context this means celebrating. Upon completing a semester of school, publishing your book, being promoted, or having a birthday, celebrate the good work, it's God's gift to you.

Provision to Ponder

This is my broom tree. The activities listed are the activities that bring me life. Often during intensely stressful times, I find myself so overwhelmed that I can't remember what I enjoy. The broom tree activity becomes an invaluable resource to help me move from stressed and surviving to relaxed and living.

Andrea's Broom Tree

On the previous page you will find an example of my broom tree. Before you move on, take a few moments to create a broom tree for yourself. List all the activities that bring you life. Next add the places, people, and activities that help you rest.

🕊 What does your safe place look like?

🕊 Where do you go to recover and rejuvenate, seek shelter and cover?

🕊 When was the last time you visited your broom tree?

Chapter 9

Hearing God's Voice

Elijah slept, ate, slept again, ate again and then was given his next direction. He was directed to go to the Mountain of the Lord and wait for God. This was a long, arduous journey. He again traveled alone through the wilderness. The wilderness was the desert. It was dangerous not only because of the wild animals, but also because of the marauders. It was difficult terrain.

Then Elijah came upon the Mountain of the Lord. His muscles must have screamed in rebellion. After walking for 40 days he now had to move upwards, traveling hand over hand, grabbing at rocks, roots, whatever he could find to hoist his body up the mountain. Once Elijah reached the mountain top, God had promised to speak.

First, came the wind. It whipped the brush, turned up the sand, and shook the rocks. But God's voice was not in the wind. Next, there was a violent earthquake. The rumble turned up gravel and cracked the ground. Elijah stood still. But God was not in the earthquake. Then, there was a fire, a hot blaze that Elijah could feel from inside the cave, the smoke billowing and blocking his view. But God was not in the fire.

Finally, there came a gentle whisper. A still small voice spoke! In the *New Testament* God's Spirit was left for the people following the crucifixion and resurrection of Christ. But the Spirit was present far before it filled the locked room full of disciples in the first century. During the creation story the Spirit hovered over the deep, indicating that the Spirit was an intimate part of God's Trinitarian self from the very beginning. I believe it is the Spirit that prepared Elijah to see God. The still small voice is that feeling deep within your gut that moves you to talk with someone, pick up the phone to call an old friend, pray for the name that keeps racing across your mind. The still small voice of God is a gentle whisper that will not compete with the idols of this world. The gentle whisper does not raise its volume a single decibel to get your attention. It comes from a place of recognition of God. It comes from a place of humility that I am not God—a place where the hearer is ready to listen and attend to the words being said. The voice comes from a place of knowing, a place where the hearer recognizes this is a holy moment; one that should be respected, revered, and responded to.

One night I received a text from a friend who sounded desperate. I had an eerie feeling in my gut that she was unsafe. I called her. She didn't answer. I prayed and the feeling didn't leave me. I was a young mom of young children and I didn't really leave the house at night. I told my husband that I believed I was supposed to go to her. With his blessing I drove to her house. While I drove, I prayed and prayed and prayed. I called my doctor friend for advice on what steps to take if she was suicidal. When I arrived my friend was lying on her bed. She was physically safe, but emotionally devastated. I crawled into her queen size bed and lay next to her. There were no words. I just held her. There was no need for words. The presence of God gave me the peace to be present. My presence was an angel touch for my friend. Listening to the Spirit's still small voice saved her life and gave me life.

God invited Elijah to the mouth of the cave. God had promised to come by. Elijah covered his head in reverence and journeyed out of the cave. There God spoke: *What are you doing here Elijah?*

Elijah's answer is defensive: *God I have served you, I have given you everything. There is no one left, I am the only one following you.*

And God says: *What are you doing here Elijah?*

And Elijah began his soliloquy again as if God didn't hear him the first time.

And God said: *Andrea, what are you doing here?*

I replied: *But God I have given up everything for you. I am home raising these children. I am helping my husband pastor this church. I have opened my home. I have laid everything down.*

And God said: *Andrea, what are you doing here?*

And I replied: *God, I am giving more than 100%. I am driving an old car. My house needs paint. We have given up vacations. I am trying to do your will.*

And God said: *Andrea, what are you doing here?*

And finally I said: *I just don't want to feel like this. This isn't what I bargained for. It is too hard. I didn't think it would be like this.*

And God brought comfort. I wonder if God asked Elijah and me what we were doing there because we were looking for something different from the path He set out for us. Or were we looking for an answer that was contrary to His nature? God's path is counter-cultural. His way led Jesus to the cross. So, when we seek His voice, His direction, His comfort, His way will be in harmony with His nature. His way is simple, but not easy.

God asked Elijah: *What are you doing here?*

He didn't ask: *Are you here to defend yourself? Are you here to make a case for your value or seek recognition of your service? Or are you here to hear from me?*

God didn't argue with Elijah. He didn't validate Elijah's journey. He simply asked: *Have you come to be with me?*

After writing these paragraphs a hush has fallen over my own spirit as I realize often I come to God with a list of things I want Him to explain, questions for Him to answer, and things I need Him to do for me. And God asks only for my presence.

When I set out to church plant with my husband, we had a spoken dream. I wanted to be part of a community where we could share our story, a place where we could be authentic on our journey. Our church mission statement was:

Fellowship is about gathering the scattered pieces of broken lives, and through the healing power of a relationship with Jesus Christ, re-assembling life!

I truly believed that by offering a safe place for people to share, to heal, and to grow—we would grow as a church. When we started the church I also had an unspoken expectation that our church would grow and we would have a big staff, and my husband's salary would increase commensurately.

When my path crossed with Elijah, I was tired. I resonated deeply with Elijah's sentiments at the broom tree. I didn't want to die; I just wanted the hard part of life to be over. It was a surprise to hear the angel give Elijah permission to care for himself. That must mean God was giving me permission to stop long enough to eat, drink, and sleep. If Elijah could be frustrated enough to want to die and God's provision was an angel that provided food, drink, and rest—a Sabbath—then surely I had permission to express what I was truly feeling. It was OK to let it out and to stop.

The angel touch at the broom tree was actually a time of regrouping for Elijah that led him to a new spiritual depth with God, the next level of trust for the conversation on Mount Horeb. My Mount Horeb was the mirror. It was like the day I stood looking in the mirror, only to see a reflection I didn't appreciate. After my *meet my maker moment*, I found myself standing in my kitchen on the stone cold tile floor with the realization that I was not OK. I asked a question similar to what God asked Elijah: *What am I doing here?*

It was easy to list all the things I had done. My complaints came rushing out like a waterfall, all things that hadn't gone my way. It was easy to play the victim. What a comfort to see that the legendary prophet, who has been quoted for thousands of years, would lead with his accomplishments—and that God would ask: *What are you doing here?*

It was the question: *What are you doing here?* that led to my greatest personal breakthrough and opened me up for one of the greatest adventures of my life. That day in my kitchen I invited God to do therapy in me. He gave me permission to feel my pain and express my hurt. I began to use all the clinical skills I had mothballed for a while and apply them to the question: *What are you doing here, Andrea?*

It was a God question. It was a deep soul searching question. All of the things that were supposed to bring me satisfaction, wholeness, and peace were now causing me pain, anguish, and frustration. All I wanted in my 20s was to get married. All I wanted in my 30s was to have more kids. And now all I wanted was to have more money and a clean house. All of which was elusive. Funny, when I was 20, I was happy to be poor and in love. During my early 30s I wanted a bigger family and to be a stay-at-home mom. Now in my late 30s I wanted more sleep, some private time, a tidy life, a job that provided more resources and peace.

So God asked me just like Elijah to answer the question: *What are you doing here?*

In order to answer that question well, I had to do the hard work of self-discovery. The journey began with REALIZING. Through coloring my *Who Am I?* drawing, I got a bird's eye view of how I was doing. There was something about coloring that brought a childlike freedom to express myself. REFLECT. I sat back and took in my picture. What did the colors mean? What was I holding in and not expressing even to myself? The picture was liberating and convicting. And it helped me to take the next step. RECONCILE. The circles activity was vulnerable and revealing. Taking an honest look at my relationships—the good, the bad, and the ugly—revealed a lot of gaps. It revealed a lot of taking and not so much giving. And the process of drawing arrows to reconcile my relationships was liberating. It was the next step toward answering the question: *What are you doing here, Andrea?*

It took all three of these steps before I could REST. My deep breath in and slow breath out happened after I had taken an authentic look at my life. And then God said: *RE-ENGAGE.*

God brought His perfect *Provision* and *Protection* once again. God reminded Elijah that he was not alone. He directed Elijah to 2000 God-following Israelites. He gave Elijah direction. And finally, He gave Elijah a companion for the journey, Elisha. When Elijah got real with God, He directed Elijah to what he needed and wanted.

When I got honest with God and told Him that things weren't working out the way I expected—when I got real with who I was and how my gifts were being used or not used—God invited me to engage my whole self: share my story. He invited me to write it all down and share it with others. And He invited me to say: *YES.*

In the spirit of *YES*, I began the vulnerable process of writing *The Elijah Project*. Once it was written, I began to share it with women and men of all ages. I taught large groups, small classes, and even created a video teaching. I would have butterflies when I got on stage. I would take a long nap when I was done. Yet, I was propelled forward by people resonating with the beautiful honesty of Elijah's story. God's word recorded thousands of years ago had real value for the pressures of today.

So just like Elijah—I grappled with God's question: *What am I doing here?* And I opened my heart. *The Elijah Project* process: Realize, Reflect, Reconcile, Rest, and Re-engage is a continual loop. I often hear words come out of my mouth that I regret. I feel a hardness in my chest or a pit in my stomach that feels uncomfortable, and it presses me to self-reflect. One of my personal goals is to shorten the gap between my impulsive and insensitive rhetoric and getting to the truth of what is going on within me. What may have taken me weeks and months to process in the past can take hours to days now. The 5 Rs truly help me stay engaged in life and God's plan for me.

Elijah was a man of God. He was obedient to follow God's sometimes difficult and other times very odd directions. He brought God to a godless culture. He found provision in desolate places. He was honest with God and was visited by an angel. And finally, he talked with God face-to-face. In a time that typically called for ritual and temples, God visited Elijah on a mountain. God didn't come in the wind, the fire, or the earthquake. He was embodied in a gentle whisper. What is He whispering to you?

Provision to Ponder

Reflect on your daily life—are there daily tasks where you have not been faithful to God's instructions: telling the truth at work, sharing a feeling with your spouse, sharing a true apology with a loved one. Consider an apology where you don't just say sorry for getting caught, but take responsibility for your part in the wrong.

What was the last thing you know God told you to do?

Think beyond the *Sunday school answer, to go on a mission trip.*

Are there small things God has asked that you haven't done yet?

Sketch out an action plan to step in the direction of God's nudge.

Afterward: Catching Faith

Two years after writing *The Elijah Project* God came through a phone call. My sister called to share about a business meeting she had with her executive producer. He had shared that what was hot for movies this coming year was: dragons and faith-based. My sister called and asked me to consult on a faith-based script.

I remember getting off the phone and Googling faith-based movies. The most successful movies at that time had been *Fireproof* and *Courageous* by the Kendrick Brothers, and most recently *God's Not Dead* by Pureflix. The most interesting finding was that the people who purchase faith-based movies are soccer moms from the Midwest between 35 and 50 years old. I stared at the computer screen coming face-to-face with my own demographic. The people who buy faith-based movies are me.

Many conversations later my sister and brother-in-law invited me to collaborate with them to write a script. They moved in for three months and we began to share the story I had watched unfold around me for the past few years—the story of a mom who was disillusioned by how life was turning out, and ultimately was frustrated with God. The journey invited viewers to watch our main character grapple with Elijah's story in a small group setting and see her heart being moved to change the way she was doing family.

Our script was called *The Elijah Project Movie*. We wrote the movie in my small town of Chippewa Falls, Wisconsin. We met together to write in our local coffee shop and townspeople would ask: *Will you make the movie here?*

One hurdle after another existed, the biggest one being that Wisconsin does not have a film tax credit incentive. But, with the promise of a movie filming locally came in-kind donations that over-provided for any tax credit incentive. Businesses, schools, and townspeople came out for the filming. It was amazing.

Eighteen days of intense shooting, over 500 local extras, a guest appearance by Bill Engvall, and our movie was in the can. Nine months later my brother-in-law had edited a delightful movie which Image

Entertainment bought to distribute on DVD as *Catching Faith*. This seemed a perfect name for a movie that pointed its viewers to the One True God. Soon afterward I had the surreal experience of finding the DVD on the shelves of Wal-Mart. It all felt like a dream.

Our local movie venue graciously hosted a local premiere and we sat with family and friends, in a packed theater and watched our humble offering. For three weeks *Catching Faith* sold out, breaking the local theater box office records. Sometime in September *Catching Faith* was released on Netflix and something incredible happened. With the Netflix release came orders for *The Elijah Project*. The little workbook that had provided so much personal healing for me was now ministering to so many others.

Years later thousands of copies have been sold nationally and internationally including: United States, Australia, New Zealand, South Africa, Ireland, France, South Korea, Cuba, and Latin America. After this experience, I was challenged to rewrite *The Elijah Project*—mashing up the book and the workbook. This process has been a labor of love and a pure joy as I relived the story that changed my life.

I pray that you will find the story, the activities, and the illustrations life-giving and journey-changing. May God's angel provide all you need for your journey. May God meet you on the way. May you see His *Provision* and *Protection* everywhere you go.

Resources

The Bible
New International Version (NIV) © 1973, 1978, 1984, 2011 by Biblica, Inc.
Amplified Bible (AMP) © 1954, 1958, 1962, 1964, 1965, 1987 by
Lockman Foundation
Holy Bible. New Living Translation (NLT) © 1996, 2004, 2007 by
Tyndale House Foundation
New Revised Standard Version Bible: Anglicised Catholic Edition
(NRSVACE) © 1989, 1993, 1995 the Division of Christian Education
of the National Council of the Churches of Christ in the United States of
America

Activity 1 excerpted from **Mental Health and Substance Abuse
Curriculum for Laity** submitted by Maria del Carmen Uceda-Gras,
Alice Graham, Milagro Grullón, Andrea Polnaszek, Sharon Topping, and
Ashley Wennerstrom. Pending publication, 2011

**Boundaries: When to Say Yes, How to say No to Take Control of Your
Life** by Dr. Henry Cloud and Dr. John Townsend *www.cloudtownsend.com*

**Necessary Endings: The Employees, Businesses, and Relationships
That All of Us Have to Give Up in Order to Move Forward** by Dr.
Henry Cloud *www.drcloud.com/resources*

**Safe People: How to Find Relationships That Are Good for You and
Avoid Those That Aren't** by Dr. Henry Cloud and Dr. John Townsend
www.cloudtownsend.com

**The Gifts of Imperfection: Let Go of Who You Think You're
Supposed to Be and Embrace Who You Are** by Brené Brown
www.brenebrown.com

**The Message of Elijah for Kids: What's in the Bible? Volume 6:
A Nation Divided [Kings and Chronicles]** created by Phil Vischer
whatsinthebible.com

The Story, NIV: The Bible as One Continuing Story of God and His People by Max Lucado and Randy Frazee

Elijah: A Man of Heroism and Humility (Great Lives Series) by Charles R. Swindoll

Vital Friends: The People You Can't Afford to Live Without by Tom Rath

Scripture References

The Elijah Project is based on the scripture found in 1 Kings 17-19. I have used literary license to incorporate a variety of translations together in order to bring the story to life. The book does not reference each scripture quotation in order to provide a more pleasant reading experience.

Additional scripture references:

Pg 9:   *1 Kings 19:5-6 NIV*
         1 Kings 19:7 NIV

Pg 39: *Matthew 7:6*
        Proverbs 26:11

Pg 45: *Matthew 25:40*

Pg 50: *1 Kings 18:18 NIV*

Pg 55: *1 Corinthians 8:4-6 ESV*

Pg 57: *1 Kings 18:19 NIV*

For more information about having the author speak
to your organization or group, please contact:

apolnaszek@mac.com

or visit her website **andreapolnaszek.com**
Follow me on Facebook and Twitter

Books by Andrea M. Polnaszek, LCSW

Touch Stone: The Joshua Project

The Elijah Project: My Protector My Provider

Living the Elijah Project 40 Day Devotional

My Wish for Christmas: The Luke Project

My Christmas Story

Love Revolution

Made in the USA
Columbia, SC
16 September 2019